WAY

OUT

A TAOIST PATH
TO A FEARLESS LIFE

WAI-YII YEUNG
& BEN GREEN

First published in Great Britain 2017
by International Daoist Society (www.lishi.org)
© Copyright Wai-Yii Yeung and Ben Green

Cover images
Water: © Renato Seiji Kawasaki/Shutterstock.com
Trees: © Photo by Studio Dekorasyon/Unsplash.com
Path: © Sakarin Sawasdinaka/Shutterstock.com
Author photo by Toolsie Photography
Cover design by Helen Wilson

*For all
who seek
the Dao*

CONTENTS

WARNING

1. There are a few swear words in this book. If you don't like them, please replace them in your mind with "Fiddlesticks" or "Sugar".

2. One of the authors has a dry sense of humour. If you're reading anything and are not sure whether it is a joke or is serious, err on the side of presuming it's a joke. It will make reading a much more pleasurable experience.

3. Make sure you read the introduction to the book as it contains a health and safety warning stating that we accept no responsibility for your actions. It's a legal thing.

FOREWORD

When I first happened upon the Daoist Arts of Lishi, I immediately knew that it was what I wanted to do. I don't know how I knew. It was just a feeling. Daoism is about feeling so it was a good start.

They say that when the student is ready, the teacher will appear. I was definitely ready and I was very blessed to meet my teacher, Chee Soo, a truly remarkable man who took me under his wing and taught secrets that school never did. These secrets changed my life in so many ways. They continue to do so, even today.

It took many years to grasp the depths of Lishi because I had to build my understanding of the different exercises. I did the best I could and that's all anyone can do really. You do the best you can and develop in the way that the Dao wants you to develop. Everyone is different.

Lishi is exciting and if it is a path for you, there will definitely be a sense of exhilaration and awe as it reveals its wisdom to you.

Fear and stress are big problems for young people these days. This is not good. Better to learn to live a natural life, reduce fear and stress and not worry about rules, regulations or what you must, or must not be. You will never find your way if you think like that.

It is time to lose the fear and return to a natural way of living, a natural way of eating, a natural way of being. Everything needs to return to a natural way.

I am very pleased to play a small part in keeping these arts alive. Just as my teacher and many teachers before him have done. Daoist practises of Lishi are a treasure and to discover them is a blessing indeed.

To be a good student of Daoism you need three things. First, you need a teacher. Second, you need a feeling that there is something more to life than can be seen and third, you need to be dedicated to your training and cultivating Dao. It is a life-long endeavour.

I am very fortunate to have students around the world. I am pleased that two of them, have written this book so the next generation might begin to unearth and benefit from these ancient treasures.

Welcome to our community. Perhaps one day I will meet and train with you in person but until then please do enjoy the Lishi Lifestyle that my students will share with you now.

D.M.
Laoba
President of Lishi International
President of the International Daoist Society
Overseas President of the Weihai Wushu Association
Deputy President of the Shandong Wushu Association

INTRODUCTION TO THE BOOK

Welcome to Way Out

Let's start by getting to know each other, outlining the structure of the book and suggesting ways you can get the most from it. In the book, we will share some of our ideas about the Chinese philosophy of Daoism as well as introducing you to the Daoist training we have been doing under the guidance of our master for the past twenty years.

We will also fulfil our legal duty of care by explaining that we don't advise you do anything that we talk about in this book and take no responsibility whatsoever for any adverse effects that result from any of the ideas or exercises we share. Make sure you read that bit.

Who This Book Is For

Taiji has an image of being something that old people do. We want to change that perception and raise awareness of the fact that our particular lineage is of huge benefit to people in their twenties and thirties.

Both of us started our 'Taiji'[1] training at the age of twenty and it has been an ever-present energy boosting, stress relieving, socially rewarding, confidence building, resilience enhancing, fun, philosophical, meditative and magical journey throughout the past two decades.

---

[1] What we really do is much more than just Tai Chi, it's called Daojia Lishi Quanfa but more about that in a moment.

If you are in your twenties and thirties and like the sound of that or if you have an interest in how the philosophies and practices of China can benefit you and give you super-powers[2] then read on.

It doesn't matter who you are but we've found that many of our students who enrol on our courses have some of the following qualities:

- Aged 20-40
- Curious and open minded
- Not really into team sports or competitive sports (the exception is if you have been into it but suffered an injury)
- Enjoy the mystery and hero's journey of life as described in classical historical tales such as Lord of the Rings, Game of Thrones, Gongfu films, and Harry Potter.
- Pretty smart, academically capable or streetwise but look around at the corporate career ladder and ask yourself "Really! Is this it?"

If some of this resonates then you will enjoy this book because we have undergone a twenty-year apprenticeship with a Daoist master of an ancient Chinese practice called Lishi (pronounced "Lee" "Sher"). This is an alchemic system of ancient wisdom that found its way from China to the UK in the 1930s.

---

[2] It can't really give you super powers unless you consider the following to be super powers. Being able to build your energy and strength so that you feel better when you reach forty than you did when you were twenty. Being able to sense and intuit the energy of a situation so you know exactly what to do next to make the most of every opportunity. Being able to stay relaxed, calm and happy when everyone around you is stressed out and losing it at the slightest provocation. Being able to perform amazing feats of physical strength using your energy rather than your muscles. Being able to create an environment of heaven on earth wherever you go.

Lishi reveals that there is way more to life than what the media, Government and corporations suggest. The Daoist arts of Lishi provide ways to bring energy and magic into your life.

Why We Wrote the Book
We wrote this book because we think that Daoism is *Frickin' Awesome* and more people need to hear about it. We'd also like more people to benefit from the teachings that our master has so generously shared with us. Finally, writing all of this stuff down just felt like a really exciting project.

Now obviously, it is not possible to encompass our combined experience of over forty years training in an ancient esoteric art into this short book. However, we hope to share enough here so you can feel real tangible benefits.

It is our hope that this book marks an inflection point in your life, a fork in the road, a doorway into a new reality that you will look back on in years to come as the start of something fresh and exciting and new that enriched your experience so much that life now surpasses your wildest dreams.

Who We Are
As we said before, we have both spent half our lives training in the little known yet ancient Daoist arts of Lishi. We met at a class whilst at University in Leeds, a smallish city in the north of England nestled on the eastern side of the Pennine Mountains.

Different things attracted us to start practising.

Ben was an emotional wreck who had spent his teenage years in a drug-fuelled haze that ended with him wrapping a stolen Porsche round a lamppost before being kidnapped by relatives and re-located 200 miles north of his hometown to get his head straight.

He's still working on it but is happy to say that he's got a bit of a better handle on things, has managed to get a couple of degrees and mapped out a rewarding portfolio career that has traversed the worlds of HR, Training and Development, property development, Executive Life Coaching, writing books and teaching Lishi classes.

Wai-Yii is a bit like O-Ren Ishii, a.k.a. Cottonmouth, played by Lucy Liu in the Tarantino film Kill Bill. Beautiful, yet deadly. She grew up in the mean streets of London and despite being educated at some of the most prestigious schools in the City had to be removed from her waitressing duties in her parents Chinese restaurant because the combination of her short skirts, hate-filled eyes and proficiency with a meat cleaver frightened male and female diners alike.

She has softened a lot and is far friendlier these days having lived in China, studied at Daoist temples, built and sold her business, which was the first multi-award winning Organic Delicatessen and shop in Leeds. She now teaches Lishi internationally and has students around the world. As lovely as she is, best not to cross her.

Structure of the Book
We have structured the book to cover five key topics that new students often tell us they want to improve. They are:
- Finding their true nature and path in life
- Coping with the stresses of modern life
- Flowing with life
- Getting what they want
- Being fearless

We have divided the book into five sections; each section covers one of the above topics. Each section has three chapters.

The first chapter of each section offers three Daoist principles related to the key area of that particular section.

The second chapter offers three Exercises from Lishi that support and help make the philosophic principles real. By doing the exercises you will start to embody the principles and therefore understand them on a much deeper level.

The third chapter of each section outlines some practical guidelines for implementing these principles in your life. Doing so is called Changming, which means long life and we will explain more about that in a minute.

What Is Daoism?

We have mentioned the word a few times so in case you don't know what it is, we'll have a go at telling you. Firstly, let's make sure that you are pronouncing it properly in your head. Take the first part of the word, Dao. That bit rhymes with Cow. If there was a philosophy that drew all of its teachings from observing the way a cow lives its life; that would be called Cowism. If you replace the C with a D then you will be pronouncing Daoism correctly.

Mooving on.

Daoism is big. Actually, it's bigger than big. It covers, explains, and can be understood through anything and everything. The Dao is all-encompassing and expresses itself through all phenomena in the Universe. Yeah, I know. We're going to write a book about it!

In making sense of all this stuff, the collected teachings of Daoism comprise a philosophy, a religion, a science and a culture. It comprises theory that is made up of different principles that can be applied in life using particular techniques that in turn affirm the principles and ensure that the theory is practical.

Bearing in mind that the first line of the central text of Daoism starts with the words "The Dao that can be spoken of is not the true Dao". This suggests that the application of the theory and the embodied practise of the principles is how the true Dao is experienced and understood.

You will hear us repeat throughout the book that the power of these teachings is not in you reading about them but is in you getting off your arse and using them. Lishi and Daoism are "doing arts".

For us, Daoism is a practical philosophy where your life and the training hall become the laboratory. Your subjective experience of the practical application is all the evidence-based research you should need in order to dedicate your efforts to further study.

Please don't try and engage in mental arguments in your head or with us or with other readers on the internet. That is a misplaced use of your energy. Live the principles and you will learn their truth. Talk about them and they will slip through your fingers like water through a sieve.

What Is A Principle?

Let's consult a dictionary for a moment. According to the Oxford English Dictionary, a principle is:

1. A fundamental truth or proposition that serves as the foundation for a system of belief or behaviour or for a chain of reasoning
2. A general scientific theorem or law that has numerous special applications across a wide field.

In Lishi, we refer to a principle as something that has been proven, can be tested and is timeless. We learn about the principles of Daoism, because people have been testing them for thousands of years, and proven that they work. That is why generation after generation has continued to practise, test, apply and keep this wisdom alive, because it works.

Sometimes beginners at our classes argue with or dispute the principles. Surprising, but true. Its fine to question. It is part of the process of testing but do you think that principles that have survived and been shared for thousands of years are wrong and don't work?

Alternatively, do you think it more likely that a novice is unable to grasp them or make them work?

Daoism is a lifetime's work. It is lifelong learning at its finest. It is an art that must be refined and refined, practised a thousand times before it starts to reveal its true depth to you. Please treat these principles with the respect they deserve and learn from them.

What Is A Daoist Principle?
There are many principles in Daoism. At their heart, they all point towards gaining an understanding of energy so that we as humans can exist in harmony with nature i.e. all phenomena.

The principles suggest ways of being in this world that bring your experience of life into the flow of any moment. They are learned through study, through practise, through meditation and through martial arts. They can be applied to everything you do so that life becomes your teacher.

They are open secrets that are on offer to anyone who desires to learn, but they are only revealed, to those who are diligent.

An example of a Daoist principle is The Uncarved Block or P'u. This is the idea that if you can find your natural way you can look at things with a natural and unbiased mind and when you do life is perfect and you will feel sweet.

An example of a principle from Lishi is that deepening your roots makes it more difficult for you to be knocked off balance. We apply and test this in partner exercises during our classes but the lessons transfer to events that happen outside the training hall. It applies physically, mentally, emotionally and spiritually.

We have sprinkled them throughout this book, as they are the seeds from which your ability and understanding can develop. The planting, nourishing, nurturing and growth of these ideas will benefit you physically, mentally, emotionally and spiritually.

What Is Lishi?

Lishi does not come from Daoism. Lishi is Daoism. It is a piece of the pie in the same way that Feng Shui or Herbal medicine are pieces of the pie of Daoism.

Lishi has its roots in the seaside village of Weihai on the coastal peninsular of Shandong province in China where it was practised by the Li family. The arts of Lishi were passed from one generation to the next and kept within the family until the last remaining family member, Lijigang, in the 1930's.

Lijigang is the Mandarin name of Chan Kam Lee (Cantonese). Weihai is now a large city of over 3 million people and the Weihai Wushu Association has done extensive research through historical records and found evidence that confirms his identity as Lijigang.

Lishi was not practised in temples but it incorporated practices from the disciples of Wang Chongyang and therefore has similarities to specific temple lineages[1].

---

[1] In particular Northern Daoism, similar to Dragon Gate a branch of Quanzhen Pai (Complete Reality School).

Lijigang travelled regularly by boat from Weihai to London on business and it is there that he met our teachers' teacher, Chee Soo in the 1930s.

The last practising member of the Li family taught the arts to a half-Chinese orphan named Chee Soo who lived in Barnardos' orphanage in London. Chee Soo made the Arts his lifetime study and founded the International Daoist Society (IDS) in the 1950's.

This stroke of good fortune helped the arts of Lishi to escape major events happening in China that wiped out or forced underground many Daoist arts during this period.

Throughout his life, Chee Soo, worked to make this Daoist system accessible to westerners, growing its membership to thousands in the UK. Before his death in 1994, he named our own master as the inheritor of the system and promoted him to President of the IDS. He continues to teach and develop the Daoist arts so that students like us can benefit from this ancient system of embodied wisdom.

It consists of a wide range of energetic practices that include Daoist Taiji, Kaimen Daoist Yoga, Daoist Gongfu, Daoist Qigong, Daoist Self-Defence, Daoist Massage, Changming Diet, Dao Yin breathing exercises, Daoist Gymnastics, Daoist Wrestling, Daoist Meditation and much, much more.

In 2003, our own teacher was assessed by a panel of traditional Chinese Arts experts and they formally recognised it as an ancient Daoist Whole Body Breathing system that he and all of his students practise as Daojia Lishi Quanfa. Since that is a bit of a mouthful for most Westerners, we use the shorthand of Lishi to describe the system.

In a twist of fate, our Master was invited to be the Overseas President of the Weihai Wushu Association in 2004 and in 2017, he accepted the position of Vice President of the Shandong[3] Wushu Association. He is the first non-Chinese person to hold such a position and it is a great honour that the Shandong Wushu Association recognises the quality of the Lishi System that we teach at the International Daoist Society and Lishi International.

How Should You Approach The Exercises As A Beginner?
First and foremost, come with an open mind. Do your best not to fit new information in this book into old boxes in your brain. We don't want to present you with conclusions but instead with hypothesis. Explore, experiment and enjoy developing these hypotheses for your benefit.

Second, be humble. Arrogance is like a force field that will prevent you from experiencing the positive benefits that these arts can bestow on you. Drop the arrogance and any pretence you might have that you know it all. You don't. Being humble will give you a shot at absorbing this knowledge.

A wise man is one who knows what he does not know

Laozi

---

[3] Shandong is a regional province of China and is larger than England and Wales combined. It is the second most populous province of China, with a population of 100 million.

Thirdly, be diligent. Be willing to put in the hours. Be prepared to work. Be OK with the idea that you will need to condition your body and develop a resilient spirit if these open secrets are ever going to reveal their depths to you.

With those three sorted, you are all set.

Health and Safety

Oh! One more thing. It is your choice to embark on this journey. Everything in this book is an option for you to try, if you like. We, in no way, are recommending that you do any of the things in this book. We don't know who you are and what medical conditions you might have.

Always seek the advice of qualified medical professionals before doing any of the things shared in these pages and do not under any circumstances try to sue us for anything you might do as a result of any of the things we say. That would be seriously uncool.

Changming

As mentioned before, each section of the book has a chapter on Changming. Changming means long life and consists of guidelines for healthy living that form part of what we call the Lishi Lifestyle. They are recommendations for what and how and when to eat and sleep and how to organise your life so that it best supports your health and maximises your chances of a long healthy life.

We pick three guidelines that are most relevant to each section of the book. If you practise them, they will help deepen your insight into Lishi, Daoism and yourself. The practise of these guidelines is a medicine that is both curative and preventative. They provide practical suggestions that will help you stay on the path as you progress on this journey towards a fulfilling and fearless Lishi Lifestyle.

A Word About Chinese

There are different ways of translating Chinese characters into English spelling. We are using what is called pinyin. This might mean that some words that you have seen spelled a certain way in the past (e.g. Kung Fu, Chi Kung, K'ai Men or Tai Chi) appear differently here (e.g. Gongfu, Qigong, Kaimen and Taiji). Don't worry though, they are the same thing.

How to Read the Book

Obviously from start to finish is a good way of doing it. The chapters have been organised in a way that progress logically and build on each other so that you get a full and rounded picture of a spiritual warriors approach to thriving in a fucked up world.

If you glance at the contents and a particular chapter calls out to you as particularly relevant, there is no harm in heading for that one first and then choosing chapter by chapter which seems most relevant for you.

A third way you could read it is to plough through all of the Daoist Principles chapters first to get an overview of the philosophy. Next, you could read about and practise each of the exercise chapters and finally read and implement Changming. It is up to you. We think that reading cover to cover is the preferable way but hey, it is your choice.

One other way, that we doubt many would choose, is to skip straight to chapter sixteen and dive into the training plan we have mapped out for you. Start practising regularly and develop your own understanding of the exercises and principles. Maybe later you can supplement your practise with some reading about the principles.

Traditionally when learning Lishi, you aren't handed all of this information on a plate like this. You study with your teacher and wisdom is shared as and when appropriate in your unique journey.

We recognise that not everyone is fortunate enough to have a Lishi class near him or her. This book is an attempt to bridge that gap but please don't become an "Armchair Daoist". Doing the exercises is way more important than the words in your head.

Support Resources

There are a number of resources available to complement and enhance the content of this book. A full list is outlined in the final chapter. Throughout the book, we will refer you to www.lishi.org/wayout where we have compiled relevant videos to accompany descriptions of the exercises.

Health and Safety

Do we really need to say it again?
Take care. Don't do anything silly.
Find a qualified Lishi teacher if you can.
Seek the advice of a medical practitioner before doing anything suggested here.
Take responsibility for yourself and the choices you make.
Have fun.
Stay safe.
Don't do drugs.

Right, let's get started with the first section and see if we can help you find your true nature and path in life. Let's go...

SECTION ONE
Being Natural

When you find your natural way, you become totally fearless and accepting of who you are. You are comfortable in your own skin. When you discover who you really are, you behave in a one hundred per cent natural way for YOU. There will be a tranquillity in your actions, a calmness in your heart and a clarity in your thought.

In learning how to be natural, you discover how to embrace life fully and be guided by the Dao on a moment-to-moment basis to bring meaning to your life that so many people lack in today's world.

In this chapter, we hope to initiate the process for you of finding YOUR path in life. In the true spirit of Daoism, we want this to feel effortless.

Like a penguin (Bear with us as we paint a random visual metaphor).

Think of a penguin who has walked miles across the land battling wind and gravity. Aware that his body is not ideally designed for this environment. Conscious that his progress has been slow and that he has much greater potential.

Sliding over the ice now, down gently into the ocean. Feeling the ability to move with ease, to experience the excitement of flying under water and feeling motivated to head in an unseen direction driven by an inner calling that has always been there.

Life is full of distractions that slow us down and cloud our judgement and consequently many of us feel lost, confused and that life is a struggle at times. This creates anxiety, worry and stress and mental, emotional and physical health can suffer.

In Daoism, your health and wellbeing is dependent on you finding your true path. The health and wellbeing of society is dependent on more people doing the same. As more people live into their true purpose, humankind will live into its true purpose. A purpose that none of us truly conceives of just yet but a purpose that many of us feel is there.

Until each of us finds our natural way, we are wasting energy, following dead ends, arguing and fighting, going in circles, even spiralling down. It is time to stop wasting energy and stop being distracted. It is time to start conserving your energy and to start directing it in a way that will lift your experience of life upwards.

If you read this section and do the exercises outlined you will gain a clearer perspective of what's important to you, feel motivated to do personally fulfilling activities and develop a grounded centred feeling, a deep sense of satisfaction and an inner calm that will transform your experience of life.

People might even say, "You've changed! What's your secret?"

CHAPTER ONE
Three Daoist Principles

PRINCIPLE ONE
Rooted and Centred

A Brain Centred World

Pretty much everyone has to traverse the school system before being spat out into the big wide world. School values thinking over feeling with usually at least 90% of lessons being centred on the brain learning things rather than on the body experiencing things. As a result, the brain and one type of intelligence reigns supreme and is hailed as the pinnacle towards which we should all strive.

Unfortunately, as human beings, we have a variety of intelligences and many of them exist in the emotions, in our heart, in our feelings, in our bodies and even in our energy. These don't get much of a look-in during the education process. Despite having these intelligences, they are not developed holistically and most of us feel confusion as we try to understand life through just one intelligence. It's a bit like trying to watch YouTube on a dodgy internet connection. Things don't flow, they flicker, they stutter, they don't make sense and we get frustrated and impatient.

Body Wisdom

There is a wide body of research that demonstrates your body has wisdom; that your heart has a number of neurological connections that have been described as a brain; that the gut feeling we experience is an intelligence that is faster than and bypasses the conscious mind.

In fact, by the time you think you're thinking of something, it is too late because your body wisdom is already on to the next thing. Go to lishi.org/wayout and watch the video-clip of a baseball player catching a ball he has no idea is being thrown in his direction. Now tell me that it was his brain that thought through what to do then told his arm to move. Nah! I don't think so. His body just knew and responded automatically.

In the Daoist training that we practise and teach, we have countless exercises that demonstrate, develop and affirm the body's inherent wisdom. We're very fortunate because the Daoists have developed an alternative school.

It's a bit like Hogwarts really. If you have the eyes to see, platform 9¾ exists in many places and if you can get a ticket, you'll discover that the Daoist curriculum is centred on developing the human being as a whole. Not just strengthening your mental energy like most Western curriculums but developing abilities with your physical, emotional, sexual and spiritual energies too.

Heading In the Wrong Direction
An over developed mental energy creates confusion for a number of reasons. Firstly, it likes to dissect and create conflict. It deals in right and wrong, facts and fiction, black and white. It has huge difficulty with the grey areas in between which account for about 99% of reality.

The second confusion tactic occurs because it is so powerful from overuse compared to your other ways of knowing. This means your mind can never really sit still. Like a monkey jumping around it is constantly leaping from one branch to the next and back again. Unable to relax and be content with not knowing it will always be questioning, examining, dissecting, creating activity where none needs to be.

The third way that head energy confuses is that either it ignores or it explains in its own terms the messages you receive from your other intelligence centres. Not only does it cause and even enjoy conflict in the head but it also causes conflict and confusion between the different wisdoms that you are able to tap in to.

You Know Your Natural Way
People who learn to calm their mind, to train their mental energy to serve them instead of lead them on wild goose chases, develop a centeredness and a presence that is felt by others. You can probably think of people who you've met and you thought "Yeah!" There's usually something a bit different about them, as if they're not being pulled in different directions and instead seem comfortable in their own skin. They make you feel good but not by trying to please you, just by being whom they are.

As students and teachers of a Daoist system, we are very privileged to observe this happening, not only with ourselves but also with our students. There are ancient methodologies and practises that develop all of your energies so that who you are, is in alignment with who you are. Inner conflict becomes a thing of the past and the way you show up in the world becomes seriously attractive. People like to be around you, because you like being around you.

Shhhh!
Which would you prefer, tranquillity and clarity or restlessness and confusion?

When you spend time learning to quiet your mind, you will be able to make that transition to your preferred state. In fact, your preferred state will become your default state, the place where you reside most of your time. Now, depending on where you are currently, there will likely be some work involved, a need to practise and a commitment to develop your ability to control and direct your attention and your energy.

We should tell you up front that as lovely as the whole Daoist path sounds, at times it could feel like the toughest thing you will ever do. Obviously, we don't want to put you off but it's important to flag up that this path is not for everybody. If you want a magic pill or an app that does the work for you or if you are someone, who confuses 'feeling good' with personal development, then this path may not be for you.

If however, you have a mind-set that is willing to be challenged in order to become stronger, if you are willing to acknowledge your fears, confront them and then leave them behind, then accessing the wisdom that resides in a quiet mind is within your grasp along with all the benefits that come with it.

Getting Centred

First step is to bring awareness into the body. Where your attention goes, your energy flows so bringing your attention in to your body immediately changes things. In the Daoist arts of Lishi, we place our attention in specific places that have specific effects and over time lead to specific results. We will get in to some of these in the exercise sections of each chapter but for now just try noticing how you feel in your head area as you read these words.

Maybe there is a weight, a tightness, a pain, a buzz, a flow, or a vibration in your head area.

Now, whatever the sensation is, bring your awareness to your shoulders. Notice how they feel. Do they feel different from your head?

Does the sensation in your head travel down to your shoulders when you bring your attention there?

Can you bring the sensation from your head down to your shoulders?

Try it.

Now do the same thing as you bring your awareness to your chest.

Does your chest feel different?

Bring the sensation from your head and shoulders down into your chest.

After 20 or 30 seconds, travel down to your belly bringing that feeling with you.

Then your thighs.

Then your feet.

Hold your awareness there as you allow whatever feeling was in your head to drain down your body and empty out through your feet.

When you're ready, take a deep breath and stretch. Keep your awareness in your body as you softly bring yourself back here.

Let Your Body Decide

In this place, of having a whole body awareness, consider whether you would make better or worse decisions about your life. Any aspect of it, big or small. Think of a small decision you need to make but haven't yet. Something that maybe you weren't sure about previously.

Ask your body about it.

Listen.

So, does it feel like there's any benefit to bringing your awareness into your body?

Does it give you a different perspective on things?
Could you get better at this?

Would you like to get better at this?

Well you can.

There are no limits to how often you can practise this. In Lishi, we use the body as a focus for our attention a lot. When we are doing Taiji or any of the other Daoist Arts they become meditation in movement as we develop a very deep connection with our body.

If you're not attending a class yet that's no problem as you can simply do the exercise above whenever you feel like it. Loosely keep track of how you are getting on. In time, your strength and ability to drop out of the mind and into your body will improve.

PRINCIPLE TWO
Internal Affects the External
(and vice versa)

Outside In

Daoism recognises the dual nature of much of the phenomena that shows up in day-to-day life. The day has no meaning unless viewed in the context of the night. The hard mass of a cup is not useful unless there is an absence of mass in the centre. Happiness can't fully be appreciated unless you have experienced sadness. You cannot appreciate living a fearless life until you have lived a fearful one.

Similarly, a person's internal world is understood, connected with and affected by the external and vice versa.

In the modern world, our senses are constantly bombarded. It is a noisy place. If we remain in a noisy environment like this and don't take time to disconnect and be somewhere more tranquil then we are likely to find our internal world becomes agitated and noisy too.

That's not good for someone who's on a path to find their inner calling.

The noise is a distraction and we need to do something about it.

As you develop in your training, it becomes possible to create a buffer between you and the outside world so that you can be in it but not be affected by it. Until you have developed that skill, it is important to create and be in an external environment that helps nurture a peaceful internal environment.

Inside Out

Once you have created moments or habitats of peace in your life these will start to work their magic. The noise will begin to subside both externally and internally. As it quietens down, as the external demands are less pressing, you may become aware of internal noise that you are generating through your thinking.

Perhaps it is negative self-talk. Perhaps it is your monkey mind chattering needlessly. Perhaps your emotions are like a rollercoaster.

All of these can be described as noise that needs to have the volume turned down.

This is a process of internal work, of listening and resolving any issues, of being firm with any childish patterns and transforming them into responses that are more adult.

In the West, you might look for the help of a professional such as a counsellor or therapist but in the Daoist model, this is not encouraged. Rather than relying on external support, it is better to go inwards and learn to become your own coach and counsellor so you can resolve things yourself.

Use the Daoist principles and practises to change yourself from the inside out. Be fearless, take responsibility for you, even though it may seem harder initially, the process will strengthen you and give you deeper ownership of who you are.

As you learn about yourself and turn down the volume or re-tune the noise, you will become more powerful as a person. The work that you do on the inside will allow you to present yourself more powerfully to the people around you. The change may not be massive nor sudden but it will be felt and noticed by people.

People may respond to you differently and offer you opportunities because they sense your inner power. This is why it will pay dividends if you work on yourself. This is what is meant when we say that the internal affects the external.

The Physical Bridge
In the Daoist arts of Lishi, the body is the key. All of our classes are highly active and we have a massive range of physical exercises that act as a bridge to connect with and strengthen your mental and emotional worlds.

When people first walk in to a class their skill and familiarity with the exercises is zero. Their coordination and ability to execute the movements correctly is poor. On a very basic level, we have to teach the moves so they can start to build neural pathways in their brain. The exercises are balanced so that both the left and the right side of the body have to become equally proficient. The left side of the body connects with the right side of the brain and the right side of the body connects with the left side of the brain.

The physical exercises quite literally re-map and build new physical connections between the body and brain internally. The more the exercises are practised the stronger the connections between the mind and body become changing the internal structure of a person and bringing greater bodily awareness and proprioception for that individual.

Crossing Over to New Realms
We feel, through our body. We sense things both internally and externally through the many receptors and nerve endings. As we use our body more and develop our physical sensitivity, we become better able to sense not just physical stimulus but also emotional stimulus. This helps develop an emotional awareness, which is a key part of emotional intelligence.

To someone who spends a lot of time in his or her mental energy, this foray into the emotional world is a journey into uncharted territory. Just as we have to learn to quiet our mind, we also have an adventure to go on as we learn how to placate and calm our emotions and later create and sustain positive emotions as and when we need.

This can only be achieved through the body. If you just read this and try to apply it, it is nothing more than a head game, a fantasy, a mental masturbation with no real change. The body is the doorway to new realms where your adventures begin.

The Start of a Conversation
Everything we have outlined above is merely the start of a conversation. In essence, it is about you learning a language. As we gain a greater vocabulary and understanding of the grammar, we can make more sense of what our different energies are trying to tell us. We also become better at communicating and balancing these energies but that is a conversation for another time.

Once we have taken the steps outlined above it is important that we don't become reliant on the environment being exactly the way we want it. It's no good if you can only access a space of peace and calm when you are in a candle-lit bathtub or sitting cross-legged under a tree.

These first stages of escaping to a peaceful environment are purely to begin the process; they are not the end goal. It is not the intention that you find your natural way and spend the rest of your life in a cave. The intention is that you can learn to harmonise with any environment. The intention is that you can be calm and relaxed and true to yourself, wherever you are and whomever you are with. The intention is that you become strong enough to be able to influence the world around you from this inner space of peaceful, calm authenticity.

PRINCIPLE THREE
The Beauty
of the Crooked Tree

The Parable

There is an ancient Daoist story about a tree. The tree was old and crooked with gnarled and twisted branches that not a single plank of wood could be made from. A Daoist called Zhuangzi was sitting on a bench admiring the tree when a passer-by said, "What a useless tree that is; the trunk and branches are so crooked it can serve no purpose at all".

Zhuangzi chuckled and replied, "The tree on the mountain top is its own enemy. The cinnamon tree is edible so it is cut down. The lacquer tree is profitable so they maim it. Every man knows how useful it is to be useful. No one seems to know how useful it is to be useless. The uselessness of the tree is what protected it. Nobody wanted it for anything, so they didn't cut it down, and it lived to be very old, fulfilling its own nature."

When Zhuangzi says "No one seems to know how useful it is to be useless." he is suggesting that we free our minds from thinking we have to be anything special. To become useless is to settle back and allow our own nature to express itself in a simple and easy way.

If you look at the natural world, at birds and bees and bears, they just do their thing. They don't try to be a somebody. They just be themselves. In following their instincts, they follow the natural flow of the Dao.

Modern life – The Beauty Pageant

If you look around you, it can sometimes feel like success in life boils down to how attractive and popular you are. The images that companies use to advertise and sell their products portray lifestyles of constant happiness doing fun things with attractive people in exotic locations wearing the coolest clothes and driving the fastest cars. We all know that these images are unrealistic and yet it can easily create a mental benchmark for how we think life should be.

The job of advertisers is to create a feeling of need in you that can only be satisfied by buying their product. If someone is content with their life and who they are, then there is no motivation or drive to purchase things. We are constantly bombarded with messages that are subliminally trying to tell us that we are not enough and that we need to be thinner, more muscly, prettier, cleaner shaven, tanned and have perfectly white teeth. In other words, we and our lives would be so much better if we looked different.

This process started much earlier though if you had ambitious parents or if you went to school. Think about it, were your teachers happy for you to be perfectly content doing whatever you felt like doing? Their role was to mould and shape you and motivate you to want to learn. Of course, learning is a good thing but in many education systems, the method used creates a neediness for praise, for a pat on the head or to be top of the class. It creates a competitive environment where students strive to get the top grades, to not let their parents or their teachers down and to not suffer feelings of low self-worth.

This kind of pressured environment can take us away from an inner contentment as we start to judge ourselves and compare ourselves with others who get praise from the teacher, wear cooler clothes, have more friends etc.

Everything Has a Purpose

No two people are born with exactly the same strengths, weaknesses and personality traits. We are all different. Our difference is our gift to the world. School and work environments that compel individuals to conform to a specific form and way of being will always have winners and losers using the criteria that they set.

When we start to think that the criteria used by schools, employers and marketing agencies is a valid measure of our true worth as an individual then things have started to go very wrong.

Everybody is a genius. But if you judge a fish by its ability to climb a tree, it will live its whole life believing that it is stupid

Albert Einstein

You are beautiful. You have intelligence. You have special abilities. Don't compare yourself with others, it's not fair on them and it's not fair on you. Celebrate who you are and celebrate who others are.

Some people are good talkers, some people are good listeners. Think what the world would be like if everyone was a good talker and no one was any good at listening. Think what the world would be like if everyone was great at listening but no one was gifted with the ability to express himself or herself.

Imagine if everyone was great at maths but no one could paint. What if everyone found computer programming easy but no one could write stories.

No matter who you are or what your skills and passions are, you are valuable to others and you have a purpose. Even if your purpose is to do nothing, achieve nothing and be nothing you are of value to the world.

In another version of the story of the crooked tree, a traveller was chatting with the Daoist philosopher Zhuangzi.

Huizi said to Zhuangzi, "This old tree is so crooked and rough that it is useless for lumber. In the same way, your teachings have no practical use."

Zhuangzi replied, "This tree may be useless as lumber, but you could rest in the gentle shade of its big branches or admire its rustic character. It only seems useless to you because you want to turn it into something else and don't know how to appreciate it for what it is. My teachings are like this."

Be like Zhuangzi. Don't judge yourself or others; appreciate them for who they are.

Onions

Depending on how many times the earth has circled the sun since you were born and depending on the nature of your upbringing and indoctrination into a particular mind-set, it will take time to fully discover who you are.

There are many journeys to go on within the Daoist arts and one of them is a journey to discover what they call your essence.

Your essence is a highly distilled and refined inner feeling of who you really are. You are closest to it when you are born but unless you were fortunate to have a Daoist upbringing, your essence is likely to have become buried deep within. The programming of your mind and the construction of your ego that takes place as we grow, clouds our ability to see, hear or feel its presence.

Over the years, you may have sheltered it and protected it from the slings and arrows of a world that doesn't appreciate the crooked tree for what it is. These layers of protection build up and set in place and eventually feel like a part of who we are. They are not. They are simply layers that you have wrapped yourself in. It may take time and effort to unpeel these layers and return to your true essence.

Eight Immortal Freaks

The eight immortals are a bunch of famous Daoist dudes from ancient times. They became famous because of their high level of accomplishment in the Daoist arts. When you get really good at Daoism, they say that you transcend the limitations of your physical body. Your energy and consciousness gives birth to a spirit body that can travel without the need for the lump of meat that binds you to this world. When you reach this stage, you are said to become immortal.

The great thing about the eight immortals is that they are all different; some would say they were a bunch of freaks and yet they are all enlightened beings. As you can see from the feature box there is young and old, pretty and ugly, male and female and possibly even a cross-dressing hermaphrodite. There are those who had successful careers and those who were beggars.

The message we take from this is that there is no single path to enlightenment. There is no, single type of person, who can progress to the highest levels of personal development. Everyone has his or her own Dao or path. The only quality that defines them is a sincere dedication to their training.

Be Content

When you can be content with who you are, you will find a peace and a happiness that can never be gained from the trinkets and rewards that are dangled and offered as means to a better life. Practising your ability to be perfectly content with exactly how things are and who you are is a discipline that will bring you everything that is most fulfilling.

The Daoists cultivate feelings in their body, mind, emotions and spirit. These feelings are like currency. They have a flow, a power, and an abundant wealth that can be built and built. However, before any of the virtues can be cultivated you first have to learn to be perfectly content, calm, tranquil and peaceful.

Residing in this default state allows you to give birth to new qualities and feelings that simply cannot be experienced if you are busy chasing after thousands of things in the material world. Accepting who you are, doing the work to find your essence, discovering and expressing your natural way, that is the authentic path to perfection.

CHAPTER TWO
Three Lishi Exercises

In this chapter we outline three exercises for you to do that will help you find your inner nature. We are just going to provide the instructions for the exercises. It is up to you to practise and discover the connections between the exercises and the philosophy we've shared with you.

Don't be overly concerned about the philosophy.

Just do the exercises.

The doing counts and brings the most benefit.

EXERCISE 1
9 Points of Contact

A popular quote from the Daodejing is that "A journey of a thousand miles starts with a single step". Whilst this is true and a profoundly insightful and useful statement, it is only one possible translation of the text. A lesser well-known translation is that "A journey of a thousand miles starts beneath your feet".

A lot of Daoist writing is written as a code that can only truly be understood by other Daoists. This is one of the problems with academics, who are not practitioners of Daoism, translating and publishing texts. Their translations are filtered through their understanding. If they have not had a Daoist training in the practise and application of Daoist principles then it makes it almost impossible to give an informed interpretation of the texts.

Our interpretation of what is being suggested by Laozi is that the long journey of self-realisation begins by connecting with the earth. The foundation of all Daoist practise is to be able to ground yourself and connect with mother earth.

Learning to do this helps to ground you to where you are and who you are. It gives you a greater sense of current reality. It is a form of mindfulness that brings your energy and awareness to the tiny physical space where your body connects with the entire planet.
In Traditional Chinese Medicine (TCM), the feet are the source of key energy points that access the major meridians (energy channels) that connect with the key organs.

The feet are therefore very important for maintaining good internal health. Learning to maintain your health throughout your life is a journey of a thousand miles.

In Lishi, we recognise that each foot touches the floor at 9 points of contact. We practise bringing our awareness to these 9 points and ensuring that they are strongly connected with the earth at all times.

The 9 points are:
- Your heel
- The ball of your foot by your big toe
- The ball of your foot by your little toe
- The little toe edge of your foot and
- Each of your five toes

Start to become aware of these points now. Plant both feet firmly on the floor and start by using your mind to softly relax the heel of your foot into the floor. Next, do the same with the big and little ball of your foot just behind the start of your big and little toes. Next, softly relax the little toe edge of your foot into the floor along the full length of each foot. You should be feeling a bit more rooted and connected to the ground now.

Finally, take each of your toes and push them downwards keeping them relaxed. You can imagine each of the 9 points of contact as suckers that are gripping the floor. If you do a really good job of it, it should feel like you can't slide your feet because they're totally stuck to the floor.

If you find that you can no longer lift either foot off the floor then you've probably overdone it and we suggest ringing the emergency services for assistance.

When you've got the hang of this, you should aim to practise whenever you can. If you are sitting on a chair, you can place your feet flat and strengthen the connection that each point of contact has with the floor. Same thing if you are standing.

When you have the hang of this, you can start to use it with every step that you take so you gain an ability to quickly root and connect yourself with every step. Think of it as a form of mindful walking and in time, you will notice that your energy is much more grounded and you feel a lot more stable.

What is firmly rooted,
cannot be pulled out

Laozi

EXERCISE 2
Dantian

Dantian means field of elixir and it is an energy centre that exists about an inch below and behind your belly button. In western physiology, it could be described as your centre of balance (although its way more than that). It is a point on your body that if you concentrate on will bring huge benefits in terms of how grounded and centred you feel.

To help bring awareness to your Dantian we are going to start with something we call lower section breathing. Most people tend to breathe solely in the high chest area of their body but in Lishi, we develop something called three sectional breathing. It is similar to the Western idea of diaphragmatic breathing.

We will start today with the first section which is the lower section.

Place both your hands on the area immediately below your bellybutton. Let them rest there and bring your awareness to that slight feeling of pressure.

Now, without trying or controlling, just observe the breath as it comes in and out on its own. When you have that natural rhythm going on its own, choose to let the breath sink down towards your belly on your next in-breath. You are aiming to feel a slight expansion of the belly as the breath sinks and pushes outwards towards your hands.

As you breathe out, allow the belly to contract back again to its natural state. Continue this process of breathing in and out simply allowing the breath to sink down into your Dantian area.

Do not worry if you don't get it immediately. It can take time to teach your muscles to relax enough for this to happen. We want to return to breathing the way a baby does but if you think about how many years you've been breathing with no conscious awareness of it, it might take a little time to re-train your muscles and learn to breathe properly. It is OK; you have the rest of your life to practise.

If you are starting to get the hang of it then let's go to the next stage, which is to stand up with the feet hip width apart and parallel with toes pointing forwards.

Keep the lower section breathing going with the hands on the Dantian and connect the 9 points of contact to the ground.

Stand in this position for 30-90 seconds just enjoying the feeling of sinking the breath into the Dantian. As you become more aware of this area, you can gently rock slightly forwards and backwards by keeping the feet firmly rooted and allowing the hips to move towards the toes and then back towards the heels. The 9 points should remain in contact at all times with the breath soft, relaxed, and deep as it drops to the Dantian on the in-breath and empties on the out-breath.

When you have a feeling of being both rooted and of moving from the Dantian, allow the movements to get a little bigger until you feel the need to take a step forwards in order to maintain your balance. Take a step and then continue to walk.

Avoid walking in the way you always have. Instead, keep your awareness in the Dantian and move from that point at your centre. It might feel a bit strange at first but stick with it.

Feel yourself connected with the earth and your centre of gravity low, breathing into your Dantian as you walk naturally.

The great thing about this is there are so many opportunities to practise throughout your day. Whether you are sitting or standing, your boss can pay you to do your training and improve your ability to be centred. Great!

You should also practise this lower section breathing before bed as you fall asleep.

Simply lay flat on your back, with your hands resting on the Dantian and practise the relaxed lower section breathing. Gradually slow the breath whilst keeping it deep and you will feel yourself relaxing and drifting off to sleep in no time.

In time, we will add a guided recording of this process to the resources section of the website. You can subscribe to receive updates at lishi.org/wayoutupdates

EXERCISE 3
Standing Qigong

Building on the previous two exercises, we will now do some standing qigong.

Either you can do this in bear stance, which is where you stand with your feet parallel, hip width apart and toes pointing forward or you can do it in horse stance. In horse stance, you take your feet wider than shoulder width apart and bend your knees until you can feel your muscles are working.

Whichever stance you choose, always start by rooting in to the 9 points of contact on each foot then bringing your breath into the lower section and dropping your awareness to your Dantian.

Hold this stance stable as you raise your arms in front of you and point the fingers of one hand towards the fingers of the other hand as if you are holding a big barrel in front of you.

We will work on posture later in the book but for now simply lengthen your spine and tuck your chin in slightly. Look down the bridge of your nose towards your Dantian and gently close your eyes until there is just a slit of light. You shouldn't be able to see anything but you shouldn't be in complete darkness.

Keep the breath relaxed and slow into that lower section and hold the position for as long as you can. Aim for 30 seconds to start with and then over the days and weeks aim to increase to a minute then 2 minutes and so on. Some Masters will stand for hours but we don't suggest trying that just yet.

As you stand and maintain the posture, keep 9 points of contact firmly rooted, your breath slow and deep, your awareness in your Dantian and when any tension creeps in simply relax it.

The more you practise this, the faster your body will become conditioned to it.

As your body becomes stronger, the feelings of tension will disperse and your mind will start to clear. Before long, what starts as an agonising torture is transformed into a blissful pastime that you find yourself looking forward to doing every day.

Not everyone will make it that far but for those that do, it is worth the effort.

We wrote a blog about different types of qigong and it includes a video you may find useful. You can find it at lishi.org/qigong/

CHAPTER THREE
Three Changming Lifestyle Recommendations

CHANGMING 1
Like Attracts

A New Journey
The Dao or in English, "the way", is sometimes referred to as "the path". It implies that life is a journey.

On any journey, you will encounter forks in the path. That is exactly where you find yourself now.

A decision to make a change to your lifestyle is a choice to go in a new direction. It is the start of a new adventure and as such, it is worth considering how to maximise your ability to traverse the terrain safely and with strength. It is possible that the journey will be difficult at times and so we need to think about how can we best prepare for any difficulties we might encounter on the road.

Out With the Old And In With the New
What got you here won't necessarily get you to where you want to be. In order to change your experience of life, in order to discover your natural way it is likely that you will have to break old habits and embrace new ones. These might be physical habits such as smoking and drinking excessively that need to be replaced with regular exercise and powerful breathing or they might be mental habits like quietening negative self-talk and spending time meditating.

Whatever the change might be for you it is a rare student who transforms in a day or a week. It is more reasonable to presume that the process of change will take effort, determination, and self-discipline.

We All Need Friends

There is a Daoist saying, "To move a mountain is easy. To change a man's temperament is difficult". What this suggests is that the new journey we are embarking on will require a great deal of energy and effort.

We all have friends. The friends you have currently are likely to be similar in terms of outlook on life, hobbies, pastimes, places you go, things you eat, activities you do, even things you think and say. Any personal change that you make is likely to impact on the relationship you have with these people.

Some people might be supportive and may even be inspired by you but others may feel that your new choices are weird or even threatening. Some friends will encourage you and may even join you whereas others will judge or criticise, possibly even discourage you.

In a task that's more difficult than moving a mountain, you cannot afford to carry people who are trying to drag you down. You need a peer group who will lift you up, encourage you and help affirm that what you are doing is the right thing for you if that is what you have chosen to do.

Good Vibrations

If you pluck a string on a guitar, it will vibrate at a certain frequency. As it is vibrating, other strings that are tuned to the same note will vibrate in sympathy with the first string.

As you begin to go within and work on yourself you will start to change. Maybe you will want to eat differently, maybe you will choose to stop watching certain TV shows or even stop watching TV altogether. Certain activities may no longer appeal to you as they once did.

As you make these positive changes, you might find yourself drawn towards new people. People whose lifestyle and attitude inspires you to keep making positive changes.

It's almost as if, as you change your tune and start to vibrate on a different frequency you become aware of others who are vibrating at a similar frequency. This is a good sign and we encourage you to seek out people and communities of people who resonate with you and support you in your new vibe.

Double D

All of this can sound very nice and maybe a little bit hippyish so it is important to balance it with the recognition that just hanging out with inspiring people will not be enough. It won't.

To make changes in your lifestyle and changes in your self will require both discipline and determination.

<u>Discipline</u> is the ability to set an intention and stay true to that intention. Even if you feel pulled by old habits, old thought patterns or even friends and family. You will need to develop a level of self-control and restraint in order to train yourself to new habits and a new way of behaving. It's not just about floating along, kidding yourself that you are getting closer to your natural way because you have started juicing and yoga. No, there has to be a strengthening and there has to be an internal training that tests you.

<u>Determination</u> is the ability to keep going for a sustained period despite any distractions that may try to tempt you off course. This ability to keep going when the going gets tough is crucial to your progress.

We have various exercises within Lishi that help with this and being part of the Lishi community can provide support but ultimately it is down to self-discipline, it is down to you.

Discipline is about developing the strength to do what you need to do and determination is about developing the stamina to keep going. You will need both on this journey; you will need to train like an Olympic athlete to develop them to the levels required.

However, we all start where we find ourselves. Training for the Olympics takes many, many years. The Daoist training is no different. However, the rewards are far more worthwhile and they stay with you for a lifetime. An athlete can be stripped of their medals but no one can take away from you the internal training you do for yourself.

A Hard Lonely Path

Some Daoists as part of their training will disappear to a mountain cave for months or years at a time. Cut off from society they can spend their days meditating and cultivating their mind and body in the peace of a natural environment. This is not where they start.

Before heading off to live as a hermit, they will have spent decades training with a master and other adepts. They will have a very deep knowledge of the exercises and practises that will help them to cultivate and achieve immortality and they will have proved their ability to be part of the community.

Without that background or training, an attempt to teach yourself on your own, to cut yourself off from others will hamper your progress and possibly harm your development.

In the West, where we do not have a true understanding of the culture of Daoism, people often think that they can read a few books and achieve the kinds of transformations that they read about. This is not true.

In fact, it is damaging and will develop an individual who has both a hardness and a loneliness as a part of their character. Daoism reveres the soft, the feminine, the nurturing and the oneness of life. Our connection to others is an important part of our development as a human. To try to do it on your own simply by fantasising about your progress is arrogant and ill advised.

Find a teacher. Find a community. It is through our interactions with others that we can evaluate our progress and abilities and it is with their help that we can develop and evolve.

Surround Yourself with Fellow Travellers

You will encounter challenges. You will feel lost at times. On your own, these can spell the end of your training. If you are part of a community and surrounded by others who have been through what you are going through then this shared wisdom will bring you to the next level far quicker.

It's not all doom, gloom, and hardship though. As tough as it can be at times, there are also a great many positive feelings. The Daoist training is a celebration of life with a goal of experiencing heaven on earth. Being connected with others who are creating this for themselves and for those around them is a beautiful and blissful thing to be a part of.

Surrounding yourself with others who are on a similar path has so many benefits that can't accurately be described in a book but really need to be experienced for yourself to be truly understood.

CHANGMING 2
Food as Medicine

You Are What You Eat

Food is not just a glutinous pleasure where you live to eat. Instead, you should see the food as a medicine and a way to heal, strengthen, and balance your body. In essence, you change your relationship with food so that you eat to live instead of living to eat.

If you eat things that are high in sugar or fat then you get momentary pleasure whilst you are eating but then a lot of energy is required for your body and your organs to deal with it. After the momentary pleasure, your spleen, pancreas, liver and gall bladder will become imbalanced and over time, these imbalances can lead to bigger problems.

Your organs are linked to your emotions and so if the organs are dealing with crap then that affects the energy of the organ and that influences the way that you feel hence, if you eat crap, you'll feel crap.

First We Must Cleanse

If you're going on a new journey then you need lots of energy to propel you forward and to get you to your destination. The quest to find harmony within this crazy world is a journey.

Where you find yourself right now in terms of how strong or relaxed or peaceful you feel, that is just the beginning. You have an idea in mind of what it would be like to find inner harmony. Let's say that is the destination. Getting there is going to take commitment and discipline and patience and endurance. If your body doesn't have lots of energy or the emotions are out of balance then that journey becomes more difficult, some would say impossible. You will find yourself dropping back to old habits.

When you cleanse yourself, you will feel a boost in energy because your body will not have to work so hard ridding itself of unnecessary toxins. You will be better able to tune in to what your body needs and how to balance it on a physical, mental and emotional level. This will act as a guide and make it easier for you to progress.

Your Diet Must Support Your Journey

According to Daoist theory, your day-to-day energy comes from two main sources. One is the food that you consume and the other is your breath. You want to put into your body fuel that is going to give you the most energy and not sap or deplete you.

Your diet needs to reflect this and so the Daoists and specifically my teachers' teachers' teacher created lists for his Western students to help. These lists outline what to consume less of and eradicate from your diet as well as lists of what to include in your diet so that you maximise your energy intake and minimise energy depletion.

This fuel for your body will also fuel you in training yourself to be a Daoist Warrior. Physically, mentally, emotionally and spiritually fit to walk your life path and achieve your destiny.

There's No Hurry

The Daoists follow nature. They observe that things with the greatest strength start slowly and build up momentum. Think of a snowball rolling down a hill until it becomes an avalanche or a tiny acorn that grows to become a mighty oak tree.

In Daoism, they call this the middle way, which is to always do things in moderation because nothing extreme or faddy will stick. You won't sustain extreme change for the rest of your life and you will just go from peak to trough.

Incremental changes that are gradual are more profound and deeper because by building steadily rather than spiking and then falling back again, you are always making progress. That steady, sustainable, achievable progress reminds you that you are benefitting from the changes and that you are capable of making these changes.

The Food Feeling Connection

Your body will start to educate you. You will learn that your body responds differently to certain foods and drinks. The way that you feel on a physical and emotional level becomes the start of a conversation that you can learn to listen to and tap in to your own body's wisdom so that you don't necessarily have to look externally for answers.

Pain is a loud indication that something isn't right and as you become more and more sensitive, you might start to become aware of aches and pains that weren't there before. This is your body's way of getting your attention and telling you that something is not right. As you address the concerns of the loudest voices and they subside into silence, you will become aware of the next chorus calling for your attention.

Pains and sensations that may always have been there but which you couldn't respond to because of the louder more pressing pain. The cacophony of modern life can drown all of this out and for some people it is not until they are suffering from chronic illness that they take note and look for lifestyle changes or external fixes. You don't want to wait until you get to that stage. Wherever you are, it is never too early to start listening and responding to what your body needs.

Sometimes you will experience cravings for particular foods.
We're not talking about sugar or alcohol but those strange cravings for foods that you seldom eat. This will be your body telling you that it is missing a trace element that is found in those foods.

Trust your body. It might seem strange to buy a jar of pickled cucumbers and eat them for your breakfast, but if that is what your body is telling you to do. Thank it and do as it says.

Seven

You might have been eating sugar since you were a child so for you to make a step towards clearing that fully from your system and ending any addiction or dependency on it will take time. You can't think of this as a fad. It's a marathon and not a sprint and you need to appreciate the time it takes for your body to regenerate fully. The Daoists say that it takes seven years for your body to fully replenish itself if you follow a lifestyle that supports that process.

Most people have difficulty keeping a new years' resolution beyond January so I hope you can see that those kinds of bold statements and sudden, harsh changes create a tension that quickly leads to them snapping back into old behaviours.

If you think of this as a seven-year project, then you have much more time to convince yourself and practise eating a different way. You will recognise that you won't be perfect all the time but that as long as you are sticking to gradual improvements more often than not, you will be helping the body to do what it does naturally.

As you make small changes consistently, you will start to feel the benefits and that will further motivate you to keep improving and refining your diet. No artists painted a masterpiece the very first time they picked up a brush. Changming is one of the Daoist Arts and if you want to become a practitioner then you will discover how the food you choose, the way you respond to your body's wisdom is an art, and you need to become an artist.

Art Not Fad

It is a daily practise that you will refine for the rest of your life. That is why Changming doesn't have any rules. Overall, we eat a largely vegetarian diet but at times in a person's life or depending on how they are using their body, a bit of chicken or fish might be necessary to support the body.

If you live in a cold country such as the UK, certain foods like tropical fruit are ill advised because of their yin qualities.

However, if you travel to a hot country then it becomes OK to eat them because the environment that your body is in has changed to a more yang one. The same thing happens as we progress from one season to the next.

There are people who push a raw food diet as being great for your body. The Daoists would agree that it might be good for the body during the summer but they also caution against eating cold foods during the winter months.

Instead of saying "Right I'm cutting dairy and sugar and meat from my diet and I'm never going to eat them again" it is better to say "What is something that I eat too much of? How can I reduce or eliminate this as a regular food I consume? What is something I don't eat often enough that would benefit my health? How can I start to include this in my diet?"

By constantly tinkering and noticing the affects you will develop a refined relationship with food and its effect on you. You will avoid the cravings and crashes associated with dietary changes but instead will start to design a way of eating that supports the physical, mental, emotional and spiritual direction you want your life to go in.

CHANGMING 3
Make Time for You

Modern Life Is Yang

In the Western world, modern life is no longer natural for the vast majority of people. The ability to produce electricity has made it so that we can light our environment even after the sun has gone down. We can continue to work long hours regardless of the time of year and the natural rhythms of the days and seasons play less of a role in our activities.

The development of technology and in particular the internet and smart phones means that we are constantly connected to unfathomable amounts of information, education and social networks that are constantly streaming content at us.

This 'always on' nature of modern life makes it very difficult to switch-off and just be, just rest with your own thoughts or daydream for a little while. The hyper-activity that we are surrounded by, connected with and drawn to contribute to is very external, very busy and what the Daoists would describe as a yang energy.

Time and Space for You

When people can message us by txt, e-mail or instant message and push their way in to our consciousness, our attention is constantly being drawn towards their needs.

They take up mental space and draw on our emotions. If we have tasks to do, such as return a call or reply to an e-mail, our brain is aware either consciously or sub-consciously. Carrying these tasks has a psychological weight, which is draining.

There are not many people who go to bed each night having replied to every inbound communication of the day. How many times have you switched off the light only to switch it back on to send 'one final message' because you don't want it hanging over until the next day?

In some ways, modern life can feel like you are being washed along on a tide of other people's comments, opinions and desires.

It's not uncommon to hear people saying that they feel overwhelmed or just can't think straight or even know what to think. We are in an era where truth and facts have become less important and attention grabbing headlines, click-bait or false reporting have become the norm.

In such an environment, if you are going to re-connect with your inner nature, you need to make time to unplug and create space to just be.

Individuals

Daoism is a philosophy but at times, it is described as a religion. Many people are turned off by the word religion for different reasons. One thing that can be particularly unattractive to 'non-believers' is the evangelical nature of shoving a particular world-view down other people's throats. Although these people are often coming from a well-meaning place (they want to save us from our sins and eternal damnation in the afterlife), they can be somewhat annoying.

Daoism on the other hand is a little different. Daoists recognise they have access to an ancient wisdom that has practical benefit. Just as an eagle doesn't try to encourage a pig to fly, a Daoist is happy to just soar. She knows that those with the eyes to see, the ears to hear and the heart to follow will come to the Dao of their own accord, in their own way at the time that is right for them.

Any kind of evangelical crusade to recruit more followers is a tremendous waste of energy that is better spent on your own cultivation and development.

There are certain principles of Daoism but everyone's approach to understanding and practising those principles is unique to them. There are masters who have gone before us and can provide structure for our learning, much like a ladder to a new world, but how each of us approaches and climbs that ladder will be unique.

You First, First

Most people are raised in an environment that strongly pushes the idea that you should put others first. Whether that be your parents or your siblings or your fellow men and women. The idea that it is bad to be selfish creates huge psychological problems in people and in society as we feel wrong to act on and act out our personal desires.

If you have been raised this way then you may suffer from an overly anxious mind. A mind that worries about whether you will upset someone, whether others will like you or whether people will think you are mean or selfish. If this is the case, then an important first step is to learn to put yourself first.

As we will see later, compassion and benevolence are important virtues within Daoism. However, you can only really be compassionate towards others once you have forgiven and accepted yourself. You can only really be benevolent to others when you have met your own needs and been benevolent and kind to yourself.

Put yourself first now so that you can really be there for others later.

Get Busy Doing Nothing

One of the key ways that you can discover your natural way is to simply, do nothing.

How do you feel about that idea?

For many people, the thought of just doing nothing is uncomfortable, lazy, or even scary. In a culture of targets and deadlines and exams and key performance indicators, where stress is often worn as a badge of importance, doing nothing can seem like a crime.

Yet, doing nothing can be one of the most deeply rewarding and personally insightful activities that you can engage in. Try it for yourself.

The rest of this page and the next are intentionally blank, as a time and space for you to just sit here and do nothing ☺

How was it?

Don't worry; it'll get better with practise.

Allow it to become a part of your life and just notice the changes that occur for you.

Some people allocate a set time each day. Others just seize opportunities to do nothing when they present themselves. It's up to you. Remember, there is no right or wrong way just as long as whilst you're doing nothing, you just do nothing. Don't try and multi-task by just replying to an e-mail while you're doing nothing, keep it pure and keep at it.

You Deserve a Rest
Rest is important. Athletes know it. Doctors know it. We all know it. Yet, it often gets pushed down our list of priorities in favour of things that seem urgent.

With modern life being so yang (active, expansive, external) it is doubly important that we balance this with the yin (rest, relaxation and rejuvenation). There are different types of resting and they are all good.

Obviously, sleep is amazing. Time when your brain can power down and your organs take a break from dealing with the incoming food, water, sights and sounds of life. Research suggests that there are only 3% of the population who can function effectively on less than 7 hours sleep per night. For 97% of us, we need between 7 and 9 hours of sleep every night or our mood, energy levels, happiness, wellbeing and productivity are all negatively affected.

However, 97% of the population also have habits and lifestyles that are a million miles away from a natural way of life. The Daoists suggest that this hard and fast rule needs to be flexed With the seasons and your body's natural energy.

Most of us have things that we like doing. A preferred activity given the chance to do it. For some people it is reading, others it's sailing and others it is fly-fishing. Whatever your preferred activities are, aim to spend some time doing them on a regular basis.

What are you doing today Cyril?

Nothing, Betty my love

That's what you did yesterday!

I know, but I haven't finished yet.

A couple we overheard in the park

We've always sought to expand the time we spend doing our preferred activities.

Believe it or not, the more time you spend doing what you love, the more possible it becomes that it can become your living. Imagine that! Doing what you love for a living.

Well if you like the sound of that, start by doing more of it even if it's just 5 minutes more a day.

Doing nothing is great too. Just letting yourself be. Observing the world as it turns all by itself without you having to push in any way.

As we said before (and we hope you gave it a shot), doing nothing should be a key part of your Daoist programme of finding your inner nature as a first step towards creating personal harmony in this crazy world.

Summary

In the three chapters of this section, we sketched a potential road map for how you can begin to find your natural way. The true you, the pure potential that existed in you as a kid before you were influenced and shaped by school, society and your family circle.

We acknowledged the difficulties of doing this within the fast-paced 'always-on' culture of modern life but hopefully inspired you enough to make the effort to do nothing, create time and space for you and put yourself first.

The exercises we shared with you are designed as a gentle and easy introduction to the Daoist Arts of Lishi. It's up to you to practise them and begin your journey to inner harmony. This will become even more relevant as we go to the next chapter and strengthen our ability to cope with the stresses of modern life.

SECTION TWO

Coping with the Stresses of Modern Life

There is no doubt that modern life can be stressful. We are all affected by it at times. In this chapter, we will look at some of the ways that Daoists and people living the Lishi lifestyle survive and thrive amidst the insanity of modern life.

It is crucial that we find ways to build our resilience and not be affected by external goings on. Our ability to calm our emotions and stay centred is what will give us an edge, help us with our personal development and develop our stance as a peaceful warrior.

In becoming fearless in this way you will be unaffected by the emotional winds that buffet most people and instead will be able to set your sail and chart a safe course to where you want to be.

At the end of this chapter, you will have a deeper understanding of Daoist philosophy and how you can use the exercises of Lishi to transform stress and anxiety into strength, power and a fearless approach to life.

CHAPTER 4
Three Daoist Principles

DAOIST PRINCIPLE 1
Slow Down

Aaaaaaaah!
We currently live in a world where stress and fear is the norm. Stress is the emotional and mental state of tension that results from the perceived demands of the moment. It is everywhere and can sometimes seem like it is the normal state for how people function. Let's slow things down and start by considering what it is.

There are two types of stress. First is eustress. This is a demand placed upon you that actually causes a motivation to act. This kind of stress can be healthy as after all if we weren't able to respond to the stress of a hungry belly we'd probably never be motivated to cook. This kind of stress is perfectly natural and we are well designed to use this level of stress to our benefit.

The other kind of stress is far more, well, stressful. This is often characterised by persistent changes in our internal emotional state that have physiological effects i.e. they create tension and dis-ease in the body. If we consistently feel we have too much on or that the consequences of events in our life are going to lead to disaster then it triggers the body's fight or flight response.

This releases adrenaline into the system, causes our muscles to tense and our breathing to speed and become shallower. Again, in nature where fighting or fleeing is a good response, it spurs us into action and we deal with the problem as swiftly as possible and then relax.

Most of us, do not face life threatening danger, too often. However, the pressures of work or study or paying your bills and making your way through life sometimes seem like immediate threats. Unfortunately, you cannot fight with nor run away from these perceived threats. However, our brain and body has not evolved appropriate ways of dealing with them.

Stress, in a modern context can largely be boiled down to feeling afraid of things that really aren't that frightening. It is a control mechanism that has been used to enslave people and push them to work faster and harder. It is unnatural and unhealthy and it needs to change.

The release of the stress hormone (cortisol) into the body causes the blood vessels in your torso to constrict, thereby pushing the blood to the limbs to aid the fight or flight response. This takes energy and nourishment away from the organs and switches off the body's natural healing process. It switches off the immune system because in a fight or flight situation the energy used to fight bacteria is re-directed to the more immediate need to run or punch. If we spend extended periods in a stressed out state we are inhibiting our ability to heal and grow.

According to the Developmental Biologist, Professor Bruce Lipton, Ninety percent of visits to the doctor are caused by stress.

It's only natural
The natural world has a rhythm, a pace, and a speed. Nature doesn't hurry. Night follows day. The cycle of the moon is steady and regular. The movements of the tide can be predicted.

As humans living on this planet we used to lead our lives in harmony with this natural pace but with the advent of mechanisation, electricity and computing power our pace of life has increased exponentially. In many ways, this is a good thing but in terms of our health and well-being, there are a number of costs.

The river knows there is no hurry and it will get there some day.

Winnie the Pooh

Stress Is a Human Induced Emotion

If nobody was telling you that you had to pass an exam or had to get a piece of work in on time, if nobody threatened you would lose your job if you didn't work harder or suggested that people wouldn't like you if you didn't wear the latest fashions then you wouldn't be subjected to the stress that you feel in your life.

These stresses that are placed upon you are human induced in the hope of getting you to behave in certain ways. The cool thing is, you don't have to respond in the way that people expect you to.

Just because somebody says something or implies something doesn't mean that it is true or even that it is likely. Until something happens, it is just fantasy. You don't have to join them in that fantasy. You can learn to respond differently, to remain in a relaxed and calm state and deal with reality rather than someone else's bad dream.

Anxiousness and overwhelm are symptoms of our modern society. We live in times of unprecedented health, wealth and comfort and really, we don't have much to fear in modern life. It is only because so many of us are plugged in to the media that feeds us stories of death and destruction that fear has become an ever-present emotion for many.

The drama sells papers and the insanity becomes the norm. In fact, studies have found a direct connection between the amount of time you spend watching the news and your reported levels of anxiety[4]. So switch it off and enjoy your own reality.

Let Things Take Time and Unfold Naturally

If you can relax and allow things to take time and evolve naturally, it will give you a strength and a new perspective on life that most people miss. Regardless of what you think, life will unfold at the pace that it is meant to. People's expectations, including probably your own are unrealistic and impatient and induce the unpleasant feelings of stress.

In Daoism, we learn to appreciate the moment and enjoy life exactly the way we find it. Things will change, they always do. We aim to live in the energy of the present, feeling it fully and learning from it. Being open to today's lesson, we are given a wisdom that helps us to sense the best directions to steer towards or away from.

If you are frantically chasing after a dream or fleeing from a nightmare, you will miss this and run the risk of running straight in to what you do not want. There is joy in the present moment that evaporates if you place your focus elsewhere.

By letting things evolve naturally and spontaneously you don't waste energy trying to force things to happen. This allows you the time and space to see other possibilities and be ready to seize opportunities when they present themselves.

---

[4] Fear Illusions: How Your Brain Gets Hacked Every Day Neil Strauss. October 28, 2016
www.neilstrauss.com/neil/fear-illusions-and-the-brain/

The Wisdom of the Fisherman

We're not sure of the original source of this but it's a classic tale that illustrates the Daoist approach perfectly.

An American investment banker was at the beach of a small coastal village in Shandong, China when a small boat with just one fisherman docked. Inside the small boat were several large fish. The American complimented the Chinese man on the quality of his fish and asked how long it took to catch them.

The Chinese, who spoke perfect English owing to the fact that he had grown up in Weihaiwei, in the northeast of China, which was a leased territory of the United Kingdom from 1898 until 1930 replied, "only a little while".

The American then asked why didn't he stay out longer and catch more fish. The Fisherman said he had enough to support his family's immediate needs. The American then asked, "But what do you do with the rest of your time?"

The Fisherman said, "I sleep late, fish a little, play with my children, take naps with my wife, stroll into the village each evening where I sip rice wine, and play tai chi with my friends. I have a full and busy life." The American scoffed, "I am a Harvard MBA and could help you. You should spend more time fishing and with the proceeds, buy a bigger boat. With the proceeds from the bigger boat, you could buy several boats; eventually you would have a fleet of fishing boats. Instead of selling your catch to an intermediary, you would sell directly to the processor, eventually opening your own cannery. You would control the product, processing, and distribution. You would need to leave this small coastal fishing village and move to Shanghai, then LA and eventually New York City, where you will run your expanding enterprise."

The fisherman asked, "But, how long will this all take?

To which the American replied, "15 – 20 years."

"But what then?" Asked the Chinese.

The American laughed and said, "That's the best part. When the time is right you would announce an IPO and sell your company stock to the public and become very rich, you would make millions!"

"Millions – then what?"

#The American said, "Then you would retire. Move to a small coastal fishing village where you would sleep late, fish a little, play with your kids, take naps with your wife, stroll to the village in the evenings where you could sip rice wine and play Tai Chi with your friends."

Don't Pedal Faster To Achieve Your Goals

If you have goals, if there are things in life that you want to do, have or experience, experiment with slowing down. Instead of pedalling faster try relaxing and calming your mind. Sometimes the things we want are pushed away by our drive towards them. Be a surfboard not a snowplough.

Learn to move at a more relaxed pace and you might find that everything you want is within easy reach.

Anything in nature that's too fast, for example a shrew that has a rapid heartbeat, doesn't live long. Living in a fast-paced stressed state is not good for us. Be a Giant Tortoise, don't be a shrew.

Obviously, if you have, a lifetime of being trained to work, work, work and push, push, push; it might feel strange, unnatural, and even scary to take a different approach.

That's OK.

There's no hurry to get good at slowing down. You have plenty of time and soon we will share some ways you can start to feel comfortable with a different pace of getting where you are going.

Learning To Breathe Deep and Slow

Breath is the most important thing to life. Without food, we can last a few weeks, without water a few days but without breath only a few minutes. It has immense power over our lives and yet most people give very little thought to it.

The Daoists do and always have. They recognise that breath is the key to life and so have studied it, exercised it, and learned to use it for far more than the basic sustenance of life.

The immediate power that breath has is the ability to change how you feel and alter your physiology as a result of controlling how you breathe. We all know that when stressed or anxious the breath raises into the upper chest and becomes faster and shallow as our body tries to increase the level of oxygen in our system to fuel the fearful fight or flight response.

If we learn to breathe deeper and slower and in a more relaxed way we feel immediate changes in our body. The heart rate will slow, muscles relax, focus of the eyes soften and you feel calmer and more in control and courageous.

Every moment is an opportunity to use this practice to slow down and feel better. We can choose to focus on the breath at any time.

It is not the events of the day that matter; it is the way you respond that makes the difference. How you choose to react will either cause you to feel stress and fear or cause you to feel calm and relaxed.

Develop this power.

Learning to Be Mindful

The breath is a wonderful tool for learning to develop mindfulness. Mindfulness is a recent term for an ancient principle from Daoism. It is about being fully present and aware in the moment to what you are doing.

Using your mind to fill it with the energy of the current reality instead of a perceived future reality or memorised past.

There is a Daoist story called "Two Monks and the Fit Bird". It illustrates the difference between a mindful approach to life and one that is caught up in things other than the present. It goes a little something like this:

Two Monks and the Fit Bird

An elder abbot and a younger abbot were travelling together. At one point, they came to a river with a strong current. As the abbots were preparing to cross the river, they saw a very young and beautiful woman also attempting to cross. The young woman asked if they could help her cross to the other side.

The two abbots glanced at one another because they had taken vows not to touch a woman.

Then, without a word, the older abbot picked up the woman, carried her across the river, placed her gently on the other side, and carried on his journey.

The younger abbot couldn't believe what had just happened. After re-joining his companion, he was speechless, and an hour passed without a word between them.

Two more hours passed, then three, finally the younger abbot could contain himself any longer, and blurted out "As abbots,

---

we are not permitted to touch a woman, how could you then carry that woman on your shoulders?"

The older abbot looked at him and replied, "Brother, I set her down on the other side of the river, why are you still carrying her?"

We all have a tendency to dwell on the past or dream of the future but as we walk this path, we learn to spend more time in the right here and now. It is not necessarily easy which is why in the next principle we will start to develop the spirit of a warrior.

DAOIST PRINCIPLE 2
If You're A Worrier, Become a Warrior

Worry Not

If you think about the future a lot and whether things are going to turn out OK, you are probably a bit of a worrier. If you find yourself constantly planning for how to deal with accidents, mishaps or disaster situations, you are probably a bit of a worrier. If you generally don't trust that whatever happens you will be able to cope, you're probably a bit of a worrier.

Worry is an over-exertion of energy on disaster management. Of course, it's fine to cast your mind forward so you can take action in advance to make sure things go well. When it tips over and becomes an all-consuming activity that makes the present moment unpleasant then it is time to take a new approach.

Don't just take our word for it, even the Jedi Master Yoda says "Train yourself to let go of everything you fear to lose".

Defending the Village

In modern life, we are largely protected and cosseted from the harsher realities that our ancestors had to face. Double-glazing, central heating, police protection, technology and international diplomacy mean that we are healthier, wealthier, live longer and despite what the media portrays, we are experiencing the longest period of peace in history.[5]

---

[5] "The Better Angels of Our Nature: Why Violence Has Declined," Steven Pinker (2011)

Lishi is what is known as a family system of Daoism. It wasn't learned in a temple but was passed from one family member to the next as a means of strengthening and improving family life. One very real threat to family life was attack by raiding parties. It was therefore important to develop the ability to defend the village through the art of Feng Shou or Hand of the Wind Kung Fu.

Learning the skills alone was not enough. Every man, woman and child would need to have the spirit to fight for their life and protect the lives of their nearest and dearest. This spirit to survive was constantly honed by practising Lishi as a survival method in very real and harsh conditions.

Despite our life of comfort, the Lishi training remains dedicated to this strengthening of spirit so that practitioners are resilient to the slings and arrows of modern stresses.

Three Treasures
In Daoist thought, resilience is linked to your shen, which is their term for spirit. In order to build your resilience you need to first strengthen your chi, which is the body's natural energy. We do this by eating good food (Changming), breathing (Dao Yin) and exercise (Qigong). By practising these different arts, we strengthen our Chi (energy), nourish our Jing (internal essence) and temper our Shen (spirit). Needless to say, it's not a 5-minute job.

In Daoism Shen, Jing and Chi are known as the three treasures. They are internal aspects of who we are that need to be discovered, strengthened and refined so that we live a long and strong life.

Having strong Shen will give you strong will, determination and tenacity but to develop your Shen will take willpower, determination and tenacity. It is a constructive cycle that only you can initiate.

Just as water always finds a way, you must be the same. If something gets in the way, you go around it or wear it down. Water always finds a path and so must you.

Confucius say, "It doesn't matter how slowly you go as long as you don't stop".

In your practise, do as Confucius say.

The Magic Number

Daoist adepts practise a new skill for 99 days. Nine is a very powerful number and any skill consistently practised for this long will have a magical effect. Daily repetition for that length of time creates new habits. These new habits create new ways of being in the world. Being different creates new understandings. In this way, by doing over-and-over, knowledge becomes understanding and eventually becomes wisdom.

Now, practising a new skill or habit for 99 days can seem like a daunting prospect so we suggest that De La Soul[6] actually got it right and three is the magic number. Practising something for 3 days is a thoroughly achievable target for even the weakest willed of individuals.

If you can do it for 3 days then the next target is to complete three sets of 3 days.

Definitely achievable wouldn't you say?

So once you've done that you're well on your way. 9 days of practise under your belt and you simply have to repeat that routine of 3 day targets. Before you realise it the discipline will have become a habit and a part of who you are and how you do things.

---

[6] De La Soul is an American hip hop trio formed in 1987 on Long Island, New York

In this book, we provide many exercises that are opportunities for you to practise this. Pick any one and begin today.

It's Tough Out There

The world is a tough place and each one of us must survive. Nature is not kind. It doesn't discriminate and it really doesn't give a shit about you.

As we said earlier, survival is not such a pressing need in today's society but thriving and growth is a very real possibility. Every living being is programmed to survive and grow. It's in our DNA. To deny this or to shy away from it is to not follow your natural way. It is not the Dao's job to give a fuck about your survival and thriving, it is your job to give a fuck and to do something about it.

The reason that Lishi and Daoism has been around for thousands of years is firstly because it works and secondly because of the tenacity and resilience of each generation of practitioners. Having a warrior spirit ensured the survival of the arts so they could be passed on to the next generation century after century and is the reason why you are able to read about them here.

Roses and War Horses

There is a Daoist saying that, "It is better to be a warrior in a garden than a gardener in a war". This recognises that whilst it is true that we live in times of peace and plenty we should still work to strengthen our resilience and ability to cope if things get rough. It is better to be stronger than the demands placed upon us than to be weaker than they are.

When you enter a Daoist training you might develop skills for fighting but you learn them not because you want to learn how to fight but because you need to learn how NOT to fight. To become a spiritual warrior we have to understand conflict. Only by understanding it can we prevent it.

What's all of this talk of war? I hear you ask. Well, we're not talking about physical battle but the principles of the physical apply equally to the conflicts that rage in your mind and emotions. The physical practises of self-defence will help cut through the conflicts in your mind and spirit.

Whilst we endeavour to live in a yin state of peace and tranquillity and nourishment, there can't be yin without the yang. We have to be adept and able to be yang. We have to train this yang energy in order to balance the yin. We can't exist in one without an ability to traverse the other.

The arts of Lishi will teach you both.

DAOIST PRINCIPLE 3
Connect

Tribes
We have an inbuilt need to be part of other people's lives. Psychology tells us this and history demonstrates it. We have been gathering with others in order to make life easier and enjoy each other's company for thousands of years. It is in our DNA and isn't about to change any time soon.

Sometimes as we look around our immediate environment of family and colleagues, we don't always feel that similar to nor want to spend all of our time with those particular people. The media pushes images of celebrity and politicians, which again may not be the kinds of people we feel an affinity with.

For some of us, our colleagues, friends, family, celebrities and such-like are people whose company we love being in and who's examples we aspire to be like. It's horses for courses but even if we are very introverted or enjoy our own company, all of us at times feel that we want to be understood, liked, accepted, connected with or belong to a group. It's natural and if we are not meeting this need for connection with others, it can affect our health.

Switch Off, Switch On
The internet and social media makes it easier than ever before to find and "connect" with like-minded individuals. Although it can seem that we are living in a more connected world, the truth is that in many important ways it isn't.

The phrase, "like-minded", indicates that our connection with these people is based on a shared cognitive bias. It is about our brains and what we think. It is mental. The technology allows us to connect with each other digitally but it disconnects us from each other energetically.

Just look around you at the people at bus stops, on trains, in cafes, restaurants and elsewhere who are staring into screens, exchanging digital information with nothing but the typed words as content and context.

Learn To Connect With People

One of the observations that Daoists have shared with us when they visit or when we have spent time with them in their temples in China is that "people in the west don't connect".

This sounds like a strange comment if you're not aware what it means to really connect with other people around you. So many people in the west live such stressful, brain-based lives that they seldom if ever relax and drop in to a whole-body awareness that is the first step towards being able to feel with your energy.

Daoists cultivate a constant state of such deep physical and mental relaxation that they develop what could be described as a sixth sense, the ability to feel with their energy. When you develop this ability to relax and sense your own energy you notice how it feels and responds to different people. You can be having a verbal conversation with someone and listening to his or her words telling you one thing. At the same time, your energy can be "listening" to theirs and picking up information that says something quite different.

In China, Daoism as a philosophy is very much embedded in most people's way of thinking, doing and being. People who have never done a day's Daoist training in their lives are attuned to it because its influence on their understanding of the world and of daily life is embedded in their culture.

Life is busy in China and the energy of the place is palpable. Connecting energetically with people is a way of life and they have a far more sophisticated understanding than we do in the west.

Don't expect them to tell you though. The ability to understand is not through the words. It is in your ability to listen with your energy. Start to do that and they will start to teach you. Perhaps.

Strength in Numbers
In the West, our understanding of teachers extends only as far as school. The notion that someone other than a schoolteacher or a parent should be responsible for your growth and personal development is a somewhat alien concept.

In the west, we revere the individual and the "self-made person". We admire and aspire to the idea that you can make a success of yourself, for yourself and by yourself. The Daoists see this for the nonsense that it is. No individual success can be achieved without the support, guidance, and contribution of others. Finding others who can help you develop is a faster, safer and more fun way of achieving personal success and fulfilment.

With others assistance you become strong. When you falter, they are there to catch you. When expanding your self-awareness they are there to be your mirror. When developing your leadership skills they are there to be led. If you are serious about living a fearless life, find others who are doing the same. It will make you stronger and you in turn will make them stronger.

Seven Daoist Masters
We mentioned the eight immortals before. They were a right bunch of freaks. Notice that there wasn't just one. There were eight of them.

There is another famous group known as the Seven Daoist masters (six men and one woman) who are hailed as the founding members of Quanzhen Daoism.

They found each other and they learned together under the guidance of a master. They taught each other through their example. Yes, they each had their own paths to walk.

No two people's journey to enlightenment is the same but their paths criss-crossed with each other like threads of a rope and this made them stronger. It helped them reach enlightenment.

Now we can't promise you enlightenment. That is a lofty goal only attained by the very few but on your quest for fulfilment in this life being part of a band of merry men and women will definitely help.

Act Local

Daoism is not just about connecting with people. Connecting with nature is important to. The Daoists see humanity as living in the space between heaven and earth. If there is imbalance in either heaven or earth then humanity suffers.

We have already talked about the importance of the microenvironment on your training and practise but it is also important to acknowledge that problems with the global Environment will affect our practise and humanity too.

It is not necessary to become an eco-warrior but the philosophy of think global and act local is very Daoist. The little changes that you can make in your own lifestyle set an example for others. If all of us focussed on what we can do on a daily basis to be kinder to the planet, our habitat, each other, then we will be able to bring the world back into balance.

If Heaven and Earth are unable to persist, how can people?

Laozi

CHAPTER 5
Three Lishi Exercises

LISHI EXERCISE 1
Lower Section Breathing

Most people only breathe in the top of their chest using just a third of their lungs. This is the same breathing pattern as when people are stressed or anxious. A first step towards being able to truly connect with others is to learn to connect with our own energy. The route to our energy is through our breath.

Breathing deeper and slower leads to increased oxygen intake and more energy in the body. It also acts as a pump that moves our energy in waves. This movement makes it easier to feel and once we start to feel then it will start to become more real for you.

We have already covered lower section in the previous chapter so if you have been practising you should quickly be able to bring the breath down so you just expand the area below the belly button.

It can help to imagine you are inhaling a smell you like. Something like freshly cooked bread or your favourite flowers. Remember, don't try too hard. Keep your shoulders, the upper chest and abs relaxed. Allow yourself to breathe like a baby.

Now, sitting cross-legged if you can or on a chair if it's more comfortable, continue your lower-section-breathing practise. Place both hands on your lower section, just beneath your naval. You will feel the rise and fall of your breath as your belly expands and contracts.

On your next out-breath, push your hands strongly inwards and exhale forcefully aiming to push all the air out from your lungs. Then relax and allow your in-breath to fill up the lower section fully and naturally.

Repeat this five times or as many times as you like and notice the energising effect this has on you.

LISHI EXERCISE 2
The S Breath

Now that you are getting the hang of the lower section breathing, we are going to introduce the first of the Daoist healing sounds we use in Lishi. This is known as the S-Breath and sounds like the hiss of a snake.

The sound, the pressure created and the vibrations caused have a deeply strengthening effect on the whole breathing apparatus. In Traditional Chinese Medicine, the lungs are linked with a few different emotions. If you find yourself indulging in grief, sadness and melancholy then it causes harm to the lung network resulting in symptoms like lack of energy or dry skin. The causation works the other way too. If you have weak lung qi then that can cause a melancholy state of mind.

Interestingly, the word anxiety comes from the root word angst, which means, "to narrow". In TCM, this refers to the narrowing of the bronchial tubes. When you feel anxiety, your breath and qi are constricted and can't flow in or out of your lungs easily.

In Traditional Chinese Medicine, the organ related to the emotion of anxiety is your lungs. When you feel anxious, your breath and energy are constricted.

Often people suffering from anxiety can bring on asthma attacks and other chest conditions.

Similarly, grief or sorrow – which is another emotion linked with the lungs is much the same as anxiety as it disturbs the flow of breath in your lungs.

Daoists recognise the importance of quality air and the effects of breathing techniques on your health and longevity.

The positive emotion related to the lungs is a sense of integrity or dignity. This is a strength and is related to your ability to give yourself and others the mental space to live and breathe. By using these breathing exercises to strengthen your lungs, you quite literally expand the space available for you to live and breathe.

When you have that space, it is easier to live from a space of integrity or dignity that is not possible when your breathing is restricted, your lungs are weak and you are constricted by feelings of sadness or anxiety.

In the previous exercises where we have just focussed on the lower section, we have been focussing on helping the mind and body to relax. Training the S-Breath will strengthen, energise, boost your resilience and lift your spirit.

For this exercise, we are going to stand in Bear stance (feet parallel and hip width apart) or for a stronger effect in Horse stance (Feet parallel and wider than shoulder width apart, knees bent as much as is comfortable). Place the tongue on the roof of your mouth so you can use it to restrict the passage of air that you breathe out and pressurise the lungs.

As you stand in the stance, take a deep in-breath starting with the lower section but then filling right up into the chest so you have as much air in your lungs as possible. At the same time, lift the hands in front of you so they are just in front of your shoulders with the palms facing forwards.

Now, as you breathe out, with the tongue on the roof of the mouth make an S-Sound like a snake hissing or like the air escaping from a leaky tyre. Make the out-breathe last as long as you can and push your hands forward at the same speed as the breath so that they are fully outstretched in front of you, palms forward at shoulder height.

You should just run out of breath at the same time as your arms are fully extended forwards.

You will want to take another deep breath in now and so repeat the exercise again. Let the hands drop down as you start to fill up the lower section. As the breath fills up into the chest, the hands raise up to shoulder height. Breathe out again making the S-Sound and pushing the hands forwards.

Aim for 5-8 breaths like this. As you progress, you will want to lengthen the breath. If you can only breathe in for five seconds and breathe out for 5 seconds. Keep practising until you can breathe in for 10 seconds and out for 10 seconds. Then work up to 20 and then 30 seconds. When you can make a single breathe last for 1 minute then you are making good progress.
There are a few more details we'd like to share with you so here is a link to a free video from our online course. Visit www.lishi.org/wayout and you will see it in the section for chapter five.

After you do five or more of these in a row, you will feel ready for anything. This breathing exercise is part of the art of Dao Yin. It is respiration therapy but you don't want to wait for your lungs to be weak and in need of therapy before you start. You want to make this a daily practise so that your lungs stay strong and don't require therapeutic support in the years ahead.

Respiration has the word spirit in it because the breathe has a direct and immediate effect on how you feel. It has the power to lift your spirits. The stronger your breath becomes the higher and faster you can lift your spirits when you need to.

LISHI EXERCISE 3
Gather Celestial Energy – Left and Right

Gather Celestial Energy is the first sequence of the Daoist Taiji we teach. It is very calming and yet energises you. It is a form of mindfulness and mindful exercise and starts by bringing our awareness into our body.

There are over 100 moves in the form but you can begin to feel the benefits immediately so we'll just do the first five today. As you get the hang of the moves, it is a good idea to practise on both the left side and the right side. This helps to balance out your energy systems and develop the neural pathways on both sides of the body and brain. In a class, students can help each other out with this by 'mirroring' each other as they practise on one side then the other.

It is quite difficult and a bit dry to describe what to do in words so again, we have given you access to a video from our online course. Head to www.lishi.org/wayout and you will see it in the section for chapter five.

Aim to practise this daily and repeat a few times on one side and a few times on the other. Don't worry whether you're getting the moves perfect, that's not possible on your own; just enjoy the feeling and notice the positive effects.

CHAPTER 6
Changming Lifestyle Recommendations

CHANGMING 1
The Most Nourishing Food in the World

What type of food is the most nourishing to eat?

The best nourishment comes from a relaxed, calm mind. Food eaten when you have a troubled mind will not be nourishing to your body.

A Chinese proverb states that if a man has a happy mind, he will have a healthy body.

This is a great example of how your internal affects your external.

Stress will kill you as sure as a bullet

Grandmaster Chee Soo

In ancient times in China, people may not have had much food as today's society, yet many enjoyed longevity because they were happy and lived their lives in line with Daoist principles.

In modern times there is abundance of food and much knowledge of nutrition, yet people are arguably not as happy and healthy.

The way you eat is important. If you are eating and you are nervous or worrying about something that is probably never going to happen, then how can your digestive system work correctly?

Digestion is controlled by the enteric nervous system, a system composed of hundreds of millions of nerves that communicate with the central nervous system.

When stress activates the "flight or fight" response in your central nervous system, it takes energy away from the stomach and intestines leading to a slowing or stopping of the digestive process.

Your central nervous system shuts down blood flow, affects the contractions of your digestive muscles, and decreases secretions needed for digestion. Therefore, the mental and emotional state you are in when you eat has a direct effect on the amount of energy and nutrients you absorb.

The way in which most people eat nowadays is terrible. Quickly and rushed. Often in the car, or on your feet or on your phone. This is not a nourishing way to enjoy or get the best out of your food.

If we do not absorb food and nutrition adequately then the spleen will suffer and in TCM, this is the organ that's linked to the emotion of worry. If it is under-nourished it will draw energy from the kidneys and when they are deficient, we are more likely to feel fearful.

If you focus on the lower-section breathing whilst you eat it will help put you in a calm frame of mind and support all the organs to work effectively and absorb the energy and nutrients from your food.

Use this knowledge to change the way you eat. With each meal improve the triumvirate of food, breath and frame of mind. Consume good quality food, bring your awareness to your breath and make sure your mind and body are relaxed and in the present moment. Absorb yourself fully in the act of eating, the tastes and the feelings of nourishment.

CHANGMING 2
Spirit Food

Stress is an emotion and in Daoist theory, you can begin to balance your emotions by nourishing different organs through the food you eat.

The Daoists don't see mental illness as separate from physical illness. Emotions or mental imbalances are signs of a physical imbalance. Over time, if these are not treated then they will manifest in less subtle physical illnesses but whether physical, mental or emotional they all can be treated through the physical.

This all starts with the food we eat, or more accurately with the things, we take into our body. As mentioned earlier, food should be thought of as medicine to be used for its healing and strengthening properties.

Now, if you don't know what you're doing, cooking healthy food regularly can add to the stress of modern life. One of the authors (no names will be mentioned) has certainly found cooking to add a stress to his daily life.

However, the other author (who ran a multi-award winning organic deli for a number of years, grew up helping out in her parents' Chinese restaurant and loves to cook and eat) has helped a little with this.

To help take any stress that you may have felt in the past about cooking and eating healthily we will share a few tips and recipes.

We have seen many times over the years that learning to take control of this part of your life is very empowering and becomes very enjoyable.

Dr Tai Chi's[7] Instant Noodles

You know those instant noodles you can buy in the super market that take minutes to make simply by pouring boiling water over them? Well, they are rubbish! Really bad for your health. They are highly processed, low on nutritive content; high on fat, calories and sodium, and are laced with artificial colours, preservatives, additives and flavourings. Do yourself a favour and follow Dr Tai Chi's alternative recipe.

Ingredients:
Noodles (These can be rice noodles or wheat noodles)
Broccoli
Baby sweet corn
Carrots
Courgette
Sugar Snap Peas
Soy Sauce
Sesame Oil
Miso

Method:
Cook noodles, drain then put in a large jar.
Blanch all the vegetables for 3-5 minutes, drain them and place in the jar with the noodles.
Add soy sauce and sesame oil to your taste.
Add 1 teaspoon of miso.
Wait for the jar to cool then put in your fridge.
Next day at lunchtime, pour in boiling water and leave for 5 minutes.
Give it a good stir and eat.

---

[7] Dr Tai Chi is a GP/Family Doctor, fellow Lishi Teacher and student. He writes a blog under the name Dr. Tai Chi, teaches classes in Manchester and you can follow him at dr-taichi-salford.weebly.com/

In a fast-paced world, if you are working long hours, cooking food can seem like a time luxury that is hard to afford. To get around this you can cook for a few days in one go. By doubling, tripling or quadrupling your ingredients when you cook you will have sufficient leftovers to be able to refrigerate and quickly re-heat what you need for lunch or dinner for the next few days.

Always remember to re-heat just what you need rather than re-heating and cooling your food multiple times. Use a pan and cook on the hob. Don't use a microwave.

You can also freeze cooked food for those emergencies where you don't have time or can't be arsed to cook. Having a healthy home-cooked frozen meal can keep you on track when you've had a particularly busy day and feel like succumbing to the lure of the takeaway.

CHANGMING 3
Cycles

You cannot be strong, resilient and stress free if you are constantly hustling at high velocity. You have to make time to rest and recharge. It doesn't matter whether we are talking on a daily, weekly quarterly or annual basis it is really important to schedule and take regular breaks.

Just as the sun and the moon have regular cycles, your body does too. We ignore these natural cycles at our peril. Looking at the twenty-four hours of the day, the Daoists have mapped out when each of your organs are at their strongest and weakest. For our purposes, the details are not important but if you want more info simply google "24 hour body clock".

For our purposes, the important part of this is how these rhythms can be utilised for different activities so that we are performing at our best and keeping our energy levels high. Follow this daily rhythm and you will be working with the energy flows of your body and doing what you can to stay strong in the face of adversity i.e. the craziness of daily life.

Between 5 and 7am do a number two, take a dump or drop the kids off at the pool. It's the perfect time of the day to remove toxins from your system. A gentle circular massage pushing down on the left side of your belly and up on the right side as you lay in bed can help to get things started.

Once that's out of the way, wash your body and comb your hair. Two hours should be plenty of time.

Next, between 7 and 9am eat your biggest meal of the day. Warm meals that are high in nutrition are best in the morning.

That's right, you heard it here first, Coco Pops are not the ideal way to start your day.

It may take a little getting used to but if you can re-heat last nights' dinner or have some rice porridge (what the Chinese call Jook[8]) then you will be setting yourself up with the fuel you need for the day.

9-11am is the time when your body is in super-digestive mode. It is releasing enzymes to help digest food and release energy for the day ahead. This is the ideal time to do exercise and do physical or mental work. It's the ideal time to eat a frog. In other words, schedule at least one big task and take advantage of this morning energy to plough through and make real progress.

Elevenses through to 1pm is the time when nutrients from your breakfast are being pumped around your body continuing to provide energy and nutrition. It's a good time to have a light, cooked meal. If you can take a one-hour nap or drink a cup of tea then this is the perfect time.

The early afternoon from 1-3pm when food eaten earlier will complete its digestion and assimilation. As such, it is another good time to crack on with some tasks on your to-do list or make some time for physical exercise.

Later in the afternoon from 3-5pm, TCM recommends using your brain to study or complete mentally challenging work. Have another cup of water or tea as your body is filtering and detoxing right now and the fluids will help with that process.

5-7pm is dinnertime. Make sure you eat no later than 7pm and keep the meal light.

---

[8] We recorded a video a few years ago and have added it to lishi.org/wayout in case you want to learn how to make it.

Go for a walk, have a massage or do some Kaimen Dao Yoga exercises to activate your circulation.

Easy now, it's the evening so between 7 and 9pm chill out with a book or some light social media activities. Keep the brain in a low gear though as you don't want to be over doing the mental activities before bed.

Get to bed sometime between 9 and 11pm. Our teacher always recommends being in bed by 10 with lights out by 11. So that you are asleep before the maximum yin time of midnight.

Don't take your phone or laptop to bed with you. The blue light they emit tricks your body chemistry into thinking it's daytime and makes it more difficult to fall asleep.

Between 11pm and 1am, the body should be completely at rest so that you wake feeling energized. Yin energy is fading and yang energy is on the increase. You want to nourish your yin and start to store the yang energy ready for the next day.

You should be fast asleep by now and throughout the hours of 1-3am. The body is releasing toxins and making fresh new blood. Nothing exciting about that so sleep on through.

It's best to stay asleep through until 5am for maximum recovery and refreshment but if you do wake then some gentle Dao Yin breathing exercises to soothe the lungs and nervous system are a good way to pass your time before the cock crows.

Whatever you do, make sure you keep warm. Heat is energy and if you get cold and lose energy at the start of the day then you'll be playing catch up and not be at your best.

What about sex? We hear you cry. Well, different sources suggest different things. Our recommendation, if you are practising Daoist sexual cultivation, is that it is always a good time.

If you're a man just make sure you hold on to those swimmers. If you let them go, too often or at the wrong time of the night then you're going to have a spunk hangover and be one step closer to your grave.

SUMMARY

In this section, we built our resilience to the stresses and pressures of modern life. We covered the importance of slowing down, connecting with others and becoming a warrior not a worrier. We learned how the strength of our lungs and breath have a direct impact on our spirits and ability to cope with life.

We learned how to strengthen our resilience using exercises like lower section breathing, the S-Breathe and the one Direction breathing exercise.

Finally, we considered the Changming recommendations for healthy living that support our resilience and ability to cope with stress. These included putting you first, using your eating habits to strengthen your spirits and making sure that rest and recuperation becomes a valuable and enjoyable part of your life.

The fortitude and resilience that these practises develop will help ensure you don't suffer knocks and setbacks as we move into the next chapter and learn to find harmony and flow with life.

SECTION THREE
Finding Your Flow

Life can be choppy. We can wonder if we are going in the right direction. At times, it can seem like we encounter obstacle after annoyance after dead end. We would like things to flow more smoothly and spend more of our time feeling that we are on the right track and moving in the right direction.

The Daoists observed that flow is an essential part of life and that where stagnation occurs or flow is restricted then it leads to pain or dis-ease. In this section, we will learn how they approach the world in a way that brings fluidity to their thoughts, actions and experience of life.

By the end of this section, you will be well equipped to find your flow and smooth out any of the bumps in your current life path.

CHAPTER SEVEN
Three Daoist Principles

DAOIST PRINCIPLE 1
Be Like Water

You are Water

As a foetus in your mothers' womb, you were 99% water. By the time you were born, you were 90% water. As a grown adult, 70% of your physical body is water. You are mainly water.

The way that water moves and behaves is a great teacher to anyone following Daoism. Within Taiji and the other arts that we teach, we work to remove stiffness and tension from our body and thoughts and move with grace and flow. In other words to move as water does[9].

Water has many different qualities that we can emulate. It is a visible embodiment of how energy moves and so is a great teacher. Water can be still and calm like a deep lake or it can be powerful like a tsunami. It can be incredibly yang or perfectly yin. It can suck you in like a rip tide or a whirlpool or spit you out like a hot geyser. It can be relentless like a river or patient like a dammed reservoir. It can be gentle like a spring and yet wear down the hardest of rocks.

Where there is a way, water will find it. It is not arrogant; it never tries to be higher than anything. It is humble and always seeks to find the lower ground.

---

[9] Our teacher has written a book called *Move as Water* which I'm sure you'll be able to track down on amazon if you want.

It can be light like a mist or heavy like an iceberg. It never stays the same and is constantly transforming itself. Ice melts into the sea. The sea evaporates to form clouds. The clouds condense to form rain that falls to become the many forms of water that covers and nourishes the earth.

Softest Is The Strongest

In the West, images of strength tend to imply hardness. A body builder with hard tense muscles is the vision of strength that most fitness magazines push as an attractive and desirable goal to achieve. In Daoist thought, hardness is weak.

When it is young, a tree is soft and will bend with the wind. As it ages, stiffens, and hardens, the wind can easily break the tree that does not flex. As a person ages, their body stiffens. Hardness is closer to death.

The huge tense muscles on the outside of a body builder put a huge strain on the internal organs. The organs that nourish and provide energy for life. In Lishi, the hardest becomes the weakest and the softest becomes the strongest.

In Lishi, we practise making our body softer and softer, not as a weakness, but as a strength. We have a variety of different exercises that prove this principle and help you to work on it too.

Yielding Relentlessness

Water is relentless. It knows where it is going and continuously moves towards its destination. However, it also yields. If you plunge your hand into a river, the resistance is minimal and it parts to let you through. As soon as you place your hand in, it flows around. If you remove some water from the river and place it in a cup, it immediately takes the shape of that cup. It harmonises with its environment immediately. It does not resist; it yields.

In the West, yielding is often seen as a weakness. It implies to the western mind that someone is taking advantage of you. Rather than yield, we push back, we argue, we assert our rights, we get angry, we insist and we burn up energy in conflict. The Daoists have a bigger perspective than the immediate moment. They don't waste energy winning a battle that could lose the war.

They allow nature to take its course, maybe even helping it on its way. They create harmony where others would create conflict and in doing so, in yielding to life they are able to flow around obstacles and relentlessly pursue their goals of spiritual development and inner peace.

Seek the Lower Ground

Humility is one of the Daoist virtues. It is important to realise that a virtue is not just a notion or a thought. It is a practise and a way of behaving. In cultivating the virtue of humility, you generate a particular feeling and an energy that can be sensed.

Humility is often likened to the quality that water has of seeking the lower ground. It does not try to assert its will on anyone. It does nothing until a force acts upon it. If gravity wants it to move in a downwards direction it doesn't resist or assert that it knows better. It just goes. If it encounters a dam that has a greater resistive force than gravity then it will just sit behind the wall, content with where the forces of nature have brought it. If the mass of water pressures the dam and a crack appears then the water will start to move again through the path of least resistance.

By having no agenda and resisting nothing, water overcomes everything. Its humility to the forces of nature ensures that it is looked after and that it experiences many different adventures.

Be like water making its way through cracks. Do not be assertive, but adjust to the object, and you shall find a way around or through it. If nothing within you stays rigid, outward things will disclose themselves. Empty your mind, be formless. Shapeless, like water. If you put water into a cup, it becomes the cup. You put water into a bottle and it becomes the bottle. You put it in a teapot, it becomes the teapot. Now, water can flow or it can crash. Be water, my friend.
Bruce Lee

It's also important to note that it doesn't think less of itself, have low self-esteem or self-flagellate its worth in order to be humble. Those are uniquely human misinterpretations or what the Daoists call false humility. Water doesn't put itself above or below anything, it just accepts and flows where life takes it.

These principles all sound nice but just as mental concepts they have minimal value. It is through the physical exercises of Lishi that we get their full meaning into our muscles. We learn to embody these principles rather than just think about or talk about these principles.

Through the exercises, we do, we feel how it is possible for the softest to become the strongest. We feel how it is possible to make life easier for yourself by not resisting and instead going with the flow. We discover how to take these principles from our external practise with our body and bring them inside.

School, work and life have conspired to create a hard mind. We use the embodied feelings of the Daoist principles to transform hard mind into a fluid mind. In doing so we learn to enter a state of flow and we experience the peace and joy that comes from flowing with life rather than fighting against it.

As with all the Daoist principles, this is an ongoing practise but it's a fun one. Monitor yourself and spot when you are going hard then soften and flow as quickly as you can. You are a work in progress. You are not the finished product. Don't congeal into who you think you are, flow into who you could become.

Water is fluid, soft, and yielding. But water will wear away rock, which is rigid and cannot yield.

In general, whatever is fluid, soft, and yielding will overcome whatever is rigid and hard. This is another paradox: what is soft is strong.

Laozi

DAOIST PRINCIPLE 2
Effortless Effort

Life Energy Is the Currency of Daoism
Daoists are not interested in accumulating material wealth. Money is not really a big driver in the way that it is in most of society. Rather than revering cash and accumulating material wealth, they organise their lives around the cultivation and storage of energy.

Do not be fooled though, they are not averse to money. They see it as an energy too. One that flows in and out of your life as an enabler of experiences that can support their training, development and cultivation of energy.

Adopting life energy as your currency will change your perspective. Remove from your life, people, places, things and experiences that drain or deplete your energy. Seek out more of the people, places, things and experiences that boost or energise you. It really is that easy. When you attune yourself to this way of thinking and pursue a high-energy lifestyle more will come your way.

Be a Tightarse
No not really. Holding on or constricting the expression and flow of your energy is not what this is about. However, it's equally important to learn not to spend or waste your energy needlessly. This is another of the Daoist virtues. The practise of frugality.

Yes, frugality means not being greedy, not spending money on shiny trinkets that add fleeting pleasure to your life but it also refers to the amount of energy that you exert or outlay in life.

Many of the exercises we practise in Lishi are designed to generate energy for you to store and use your life. This cultivation and storage is hard-won. You have to invest time and effort in learning and practising the exercises. All of this is useless if you then burn the energy up on depleting rather than nourishing activities.

A Jedi uses the Force for knowledge and defence, never for attack.

Yoda

Western Hustle Is Like Using a Sledgehammer to Crack a Nut
Life is a hustle. A state of great activity of pushing and jostling. There is lots going on and lots that you can do. You have to be at ease with the hustle and able to flow with the hustle too but when your personal hustle becomes activity for activities sake then it is time to take stock.

Giving over and above in order to achieve your goals, constantly striving and giving 100%, 110%, 200% to your projects is a philosophy that is pushed in the West, but this leads to stress and burnout.

A study of 1,000 UK office workers conducted by business intelligence firm Xoomworks reveals a trend for 'competitive busyness'[10].

The study showed that 31 per cent of office workers had sent emails outside of office hours to signal to others how busy they were. 54 per cent admitted staying late just to impress superiors. This obsession with appearing busy means that stress is often worn as a badge of importance. How crazy is that?

Embracing the idea of effortless effort goes against the work ethic that is ingrained in most of our cultures. It can be difficult to understand how effortless effort might work for you but that is one of the beauties of this approach. It doesn't make sense to a mind that is hooked on hyper-activity, yet it works.

A snake laying camouflaged in the shadows lies idle, doing not a lot at all. However, when a mouse passes within striking distance, the effectiveness of the snake's strategy becomes clear.

Seems that I was busy
doing something close to
nothing; But different than
the day before

Prince

10   www.hrmagazine.co.uk/article-details/over-ambitious-workers-make-colleagues-insecure-about-their-performance

Life Was Never Meant To Be a Struggle

The Chinese term for this is Wuwei. It translates as effortless action, which suggests a natural way to proceed that doesn't require you to force things. It is the highest level of Daoist practice.

It should not be mistaken for sloppiness or being disorganised. Wuwei is about having an attitude to life that doesn't react at the slightest provocation. It is an awareness that sits back, waits and observes life as it unfolds and then without wasting energy, when the time is right, softly making your move at an appropriate speed. Everything then becomes much easier. There is no struggle, only appropriate effort impeccably timed. The action becomes beautiful and life becomes like a work of art.

Minimalism as a Practise

Being in the flow is not a lazy, hippy, floaty concept where you just smoke weed and kid yourself that you are at one with the universe. No, being in the flow, you have a full awareness of the present moment and the energy of action and non-action. You feel the urge to act not out of fear or compulsion but from a sensitivity to a force acting upon you. When you are attuned in this way, you don't have to use your mind to think. Your body and your own energy has a higher intelligence that may not make sense to the rational mind.

Learn to minimise the activity in your mind. The relentless chatter and noise that drowns out the softer, quieter voice of your energy is unhelpful and a waste. Think less. Just be. Observe. Don't judge. Feel.

Doing less. Conserving your energy. The way becomes clearer. When you act you do so at the right time and results are achieved swiftly as if by magic.

Enjoyment Is a Big Part of the Magic

Effortless effort doesn't mean that you are not doing anything. When you are in the flow, you tend to be doing work that you are motivated or compelled to do. It's a pleasure. You might be working intensely or efficiently but time passes quickly because you are in what has been termed the flow state.

In his seminal work, *Flow: The Psychology of Optimal Experience*, the Hungarian author and psychologist Mihaly Csíkszentmihályi outlines his theory that people are happiest when they are in a state of *flow*.

This is defined as a state of concentration or complete absorption with the activity at hand and the situation. It is a state in which people are so involved in an activity that nothing else seems to matter.

The idea of flow is identical to the feeling of being *in the zone* or *in the groove.* The flow state is an optimal state of *intrinsic motivation,* where the person is fully immersed in what he is doing.

Characterized by a feeling of great absorption, engagement, fulfilment, and skill, during which temporal concerns (time, food, ego-self, etc.) are typically ignored or seem to disappear.

Author and entrepreneur Steven Kotler has explored and written broadly on the neuroscience of the flow state[11].

He defines two types of brain state. The first is hyper-activity where the brain seems to be firing on all cylinders. The second is hypo-activity. This is where the parts of the brain that can distract us from being productive are slowed down.

---

[11]Steven Kotler The Rise of Superman: Decoding the Science of Ultimate Human Performance (2015)

His work suggests that optimal mental efficiency isn't brought on by hyper-activity but instead by hypo-activity,

Slowing our mind so that rather than being in the fast-moving beta waves of normal consciousness we slip into the slowed down border between alpha and theta waves we experience what is commonly known as day-dreaming.

In essence, doing less and daydreaming is good for you, puts you in a flow state and therefore is ultimately more productive as well as healthier for you.

The Daoists realised this thousands of years ago. They called it effortless effort and learned to spend their entire lives in this flow state.

Your Life as Art

To become a master of Wuwei (Effortless Effort) may take time and surprisingly enough, some effort too. You are developing this ability as an art so that your whole life can become effortless. It's unlikely that you've mastered it yet and like any craft, you have some practise and some learning to do.

Some people find life to be a drag but when you are working to transform your experience so that your life is the opposite of this, you are carried along by life rather than feeling that you are dragging it behind you.

A principle from Lishi is to do just enough to get the job done. To be able to judge exactly what needs to be done and when, with exactly the right amount of energy, is a high-level skill indeed. It will take a great deal of practise to develop your sensitivity and refine it to a level where your natural state becomes one where life feels magical.

You're Doing It Already

Pay attention whenever something magical or effortless happens for you. What you give your attention to will grow. If you focus on the obstacles in your life then you feed them energy and they become more real. Instead, notice the times when you think of someone out of the blue and then they contact you within the next 24 hours. Notice when you want something for your life and then one way or another it comes into your life without you doing anything in particular.

Paying attention to these mini miracles will strengthen this reality for you. Acknowledge it when it happens, enjoy it, learn from it and develop your ability to create the reality you want out of the opportunities that life presents.

Life doesn't happen to you.
It happens for you

Tony Robbins

DAOIST PRINCIPLE 3
Accept, Don't Resist

"Whoa there!" we hear you cry. "These fancy principles have sounded good up until now but seriously? Accept, don't resist? What about my rights? What about when someone cuts me up on my drive home? What about when my boss is being a jerk?"

Shhh! Shhh! It's OK. Yes, in all of those circumstances, stay calm, relax, and accept what is. Nobody said this was going to be easy but seriously, it's pretty simple and is the fastest way to a peaceful life that there is.

Even right now, you have the option of resisting this as an idea or just accepting it. Notice how each choice feels different in your body. Which is more open, lighter and expansive? Which is tighter, restrictive or heavier?

It's just a choice. Nothing has changed. Reality is still the same. You just feel different.

Don't Protest. Just Smile.
A diet of soap operas can easily leave people thinking that the way people behave on these programmes, which are designed to hook you emotionally, is an acceptable way to behave in real life. People model their behaviours on these low-level role models and trap themselves in their own version of a soap. Don't be like that.

Don't fly off the handle or get emotional or protest about things that are happening. Just smile. Don't be knocked out of your peaceful state by the seemingly idiotic or inconsiderate actions of others. Just smile and stay calm.

Protesting and emotional responses like a big fat baby just create stress and seldom achieve the results you want. Smile, stay calm, and pause long enough to feel what the best thing to do is.

Your actions will be far more likely to succeed when you are grounded and centred than if you are uprooted or wobbling emotionally. Often, staying calm and centred will calm the situation. It might alter on its own and negate the need for protest.

The Power of Non-Resistance

When a beginner first comes to a Lishi class, they tend to be tense and respond to pressure by tensing further and pushing back. We have exercises where we work with a partner to play with this pressure and response and we learn to do the opposite.

We learn how tension, resistance and pushing against a force is weak and in fact is a waste of energy. If we tense against a pressure, their strength becomes stronger.

We learn to turn acceptance into a strength. When we learn to accept our partners force, it becomes our strength and it becomes their weakness.

Just like all of these principles, it takes time and practise and ideally the guidance of a teacher to make this skill real for you.

Personal Power

If we want to find harmony in this crazy world then we need to develop the ability to be peaceful, calm and happy. If people, life, events or the news has the ability to knock you out of that then your personal power is weak and needs strengthening.

We cannot control everything that happens to us. What we can learn to control is how we respond to the things that happen. When you can respond to events in ways that keep you feeling centred and strong, you are developing your personal power.

The key to this is to accept. Accepting allows life in. It embraces what is and allows it to flow. Resisting creates a tension between what is and what you are able to accept. As long as you push back, that tension will continue to build and pressurise you. What we resist will persist. What we accept, we will forget.

The Daoist Farmer
There was a farmer whose horse ran away. That evening the neighbours gathered to commiserate with him since this was such bad luck.

He said, "Maybe."

The next day the horse returned, but brought with it six wild horses and the neighbours came exclaiming at his good fortune.

He said, "Maybe."

Then, the following day, his son tried to saddle and ride one of the wild horses, was thrown, and broke his leg.

Again, the neighbours came to offer their sympathy for the misfortune.

He said, "Maybe."

The day after that, conscription officers came to the village to seize young men for the army, but because of the broken leg, the farmer's son was rejected. When the neighbours came in to say how fortunately everything had turned out,

He said, "Maybe."

Source: Tao: The Watercourse Way, by Alan Watts

If something upsets you, the more you fight it the longer you will be unhappy. You put yourself into that state mentally and emotionally so stop. Accept it and observe how that dissolves much of the bad feeling. Learn to get quicker at this. Rather than taking weeks to get over something, reduce it to seconds.

Stay in a state of calm happiness and live your life from there.

If good happens, good;

if bad happens, good

Laozi

In the eyes of the Dao, nothing is good or bad. Right and wrong are subjective evaluations made up by people. Whether you think of something as good or bad is just your opinion.

If this opinion is making you stressed or stuck, change your opinion. Find a way to see the positive in whatever life throws at you. Use it as a stepping-stone to benefit you rather than as a boulder that blocks your path. Accept what is there and use it to your advantage. Do this and you will maintain a harmony in your life that few ever experience.

CHAPTER EIGHT
Three Lishi Exercises

EXERCISE 1
Silk Reeling

Silk Reeling is a set of repetitive spiral movements using the legs, torso, arms and hands. The gradual opening and closing movements create inner energy circulation, concentrated on a connection to the earth, dantian rotation, waist turning, and knee alignment. There is a lot going on in the exercise which makes it quite difficult to describe so what follows is some key points to pay attention to as you watch the video lesson at www.lishi.org/wayout

Start with your feet parallel and placed more than shoulder width apart. The toes should be pointing forwards and your awareness should be in the 9 points of contact with the earth (as outlined on page 43) Bend both knees as far as is comfortable keeping the posture upright and the weight in the middle. As you bend your knees, don't let them collapse inwards but instead, push them outwards so they are over the little toe edge of each foot. This is Riding Horse Stance.

Start to push the weight to one side until it is all over one leg. This leg should be bent and the other leg that has no weight on it should be straight. This is Leopard Stance. The feet should not move and the knee of the bent leg should remain over the little toe edge and should not push forward beyond the tips of the toes.

Bring the weight back into the centre to Riding Horse Stance and keep the weight shifting towards the leg that was straight just now. As the weight goes over the bent leg, the other leg should straighten until you are in leopard stance on the other leg.

Repeat this transition of weight from one leg to the other pushing from leopard through riding horse to leopard on the other side. Don't hold the stance but keep flowing from one leg to the other at a steady pace.

Now the arms. Raise the arms with the palms down at waist height as if resting on a table. As you push the weight from one leg to the other, the palms should remain flat on the imaginary tabletop as if you are wiping the table clean with both hands.

Keeping the hips square to the front, the arms outstretched and the palms flat on the table, when you reach leopard stance, turn your waist so that your arms can circle to the outside of your torso. Turn your waist back to the front so your arms return in front of you as you transition through horse to leopard on the other side. Again, in leopard, keep the hips square to the front as you turn the waist and wipe the hands to the outside of your torso before returning to the front in leopard and transitioning back to the other side.

Keep this motion going, taking long deep breathes. Start with an inhale of 5 seconds and an exhale of 5 seconds. Breathing in as you move to left leopard and breathing out as you transition to right leopard.

Keep the body relaxed and use the flow of your breath to drive the flow of your movements. As your body gets stronger and your movements get more flowing, increase the length of time that you practise silk reeling. Five minutes is a good length of time to aim for in the beginning.

EXERCISE 2
Kaimen

Kaimen means Open Door and it is the Daoist Yoga that we practise in Lishi. This next exercise works the Liver meridian.

The Liver is the organ responsible for the smooth flow of emotions as well as qi and blood.

Starting Position - Praying Mantis Stance.

Sit on the floor with your feet tucked under you so that your bum is resting on your calves and your knees are together in front of you.

SEQUENCE
1. Breathe IN Place the hands on the hips with the fingers facing forwards and take a full breath (three-section breathing).
2. Breathe OUT Part the knees.
3. Breathe IN Return the knees.
4. Breathe OUT Relax back to starting position.
REPEAT 1 - 4

EXTENSION
Repeat sequence, but when the knees are parted, place the hands inside the knees and push them further apart and lean back slightly. Draw the knees back together, move your weight forward again and relax. Keep the toes touching throughout.
REPEAT Extension.

EXERCISE 3
Guided Meditation

The Microcosmic Orbit is a Daoist meditation that rotates energy flow through a major energy circuit of the body.

Sit cross-legged on the floor or on a chair with feet flat on the ground. Hold the spine upright with the chin slightly tucked. Place the tongue on the roof of the mouth and lower the eyes to look down the nose. Gently close the eyes until only a slit of light is visible. Look inwards and down towards the Dantian (just below and behind the naval).

There are many different hand formations but for now just relax your hands and arms so they are resting on your lap or thighs.

Bring your awareness to your breath and softly begin the lower-section breathing maintaining your concentration on your Dantian.

After a number of breaths and when it feels right to do so visualise a channel running from your Dantian down to your perineum (a point between your anus and your genitals) and then back up to a point on your spine called the Mingmen opposite the Dantian.

On your next in-breath, use your mind to pull from your Dantian down to the perineum and back up to the Mingmen. As you breathe out, retrace the channel from the Mingmen to the perineum and back to the Dantian.

Repeat this for three breaths or so.

Now visualise the channel extending up your spine to the point where your back becomes your neck.

On your next in-breath, use your mind to pull from your Dantian down to the perineum and back up to the Mingmen and right up the spine to the point where your neck and back meet. As you breathe out, retrace the channel back down the spine, past the Mingmen to the perineum and back to the Dantian.

Repeat this for three breaths or so.

Now visualise the channel extending further up the neck to a point on the crown of the head.

On your next in-breath, use your mind to pull from your Dantian down to the perineum and back up to the Mingmen and right up the spine to the point on the crown of the head. As you breathe out, retrace the channel back down the spine, past the Mingmen to the perineum and back to the Dantian.

Repeat this for three breaths or so.

Now visualise a channel that runs from the crown of your head, over the forehead, down the bridge of the nose, through the palate on to the tongue (which should be touching the roof of the mouth) down the chest and belly and back to the Dantian.

On your next in-breath, use your mind to pull from your Dantian down to the perineum and back up to the Mingmen and right up the spine to the point on the crown of the head.

This time, as you breathe out, bring your attention down the channel on the front of the body, from the crown of your head, over the forehead, down the bridge of the nose, through the palate on to the tongue down the chest and belly and back to the Dantian.

You have completed the first circuit of the Micro-Cosmic Orbit.

Take 3 long breathes in to the lower section keeping your attention in your Dantian.

On the next breath complete another circuit of the Micro-Cosmic Orbit bringing the breath and energy up the back of the spine to the crown of the head on the in-breath and down the front of the body back to the Dantian on the out breathe.

Rest for three breathes and then repeat another circuit. Keep this going for as long as it feels relaxed to do so. Don't overdo it.

When it feels like time to bring the practise to a close, bring your breathe and concentration back to the Dantian. Raise the hands and place the heel of each palm lightly over each eye. Take six long breathes in through the nose and out through the nose and then relax the hands down slowly opening your eyes.

Take a moment or two to reacclimatise yourself to your surroundings. You might want to give your legs a little massage before standing up.

Each time you practise, observe the flow of the circuit becoming smoother. It is important not to race or force the flow. As the flow becomes smoother in your practise, observe whether your life also flows more smoothly.

CHAPTER NINE
Three Changming Lifestyle Recommendations

CHANGMING 1
Portability

A key component of Changming is the food you eat, in other words, you might call it a diet. Many popular diets are just fads that have been designed to sell books and make money from people's insecurities about their weight and appearance.

Changming on the other hand has been around for thousands of years and in the 1930s my teachers' teachers' teacher set about codifying it for people living in the West. The principles remained the same but the foods that were available in 1930's London differed from the foods he was familiar with growing up in China.

This illustrates one of the key principles of the Changming diet. It is fluid and it is portable. Wherever you are in the world the principles of Changming can be flexed to suit you and the environment.

In an attempt to make them easier to follow, many other diets have simple rules but this can lead to an oversimplification and a rigidity in approach.

We've all seen people who are so rigid and strict about their dietary needs, that when they find themselves in a restaurant that doesn't serve gluten free vegan buckwheat pancakes, get so stressed that they flood their body with adrenaline and cortisol destroying any benefit that their diets might be having.

Our teacher maintains that there is no point doing Changming if you are stressed. As we said in a previous chapter, stress is way more harmful for your body than a bag of chips so if you're going to do Changming make sure that getting stressed out is not a part of it.

Again, Changming is an art that you will work on. Over time, choosing healthier foods will become your preference rather than an effort. Your body will learn to like the choices you make because it feels so much better when you eat this way. It takes 7 years for your body to regenerate completely and so think about this as a longer-term project than just a 30-day diet plan.

In Lishi, we don't even refer to Changming as a diet. Instead, we consider it helpful guidelines for living a long and healthy life. Guidelines are way better than rules don't you think. Rules are rigid and narrow whereas guidelines provide flexibility and breadth.

One of the guidelines of Changming is to adapt it to your environment. If you are living and eating in harmony with your environment then you will set up the balance and harmony you want in your body and mental and emotional states.

In a cold environment, warmer more yang foods are recommended. In a hot climate, yin foods become acceptable as a way of maintaining balance. Pineapples are a very yin food that to a Daoist would make no sense to eat in the cold winters of England but in the hot summers of the Caribbean, they are a perfectly sensible choice.

Having a flexible and flowing approach to the food you eat is essential to guarding against the harmful rigidity of a militant health nut and making sure that you develop a fluid approach in keeping with the Daoist principles.

All food has energy. Your body needs energy, so if you find yourself stranded on a desert island with nothing but a month's supply of Mars bars, well eat the frickin' Mars bars. When you're in an environment where you have more choices, choose wisely.

The key principle to bear in mind is to consume those foods that give you more energy than they take to digest or eradicate from your body.

CHANGMING 2
Look After Your Liver

The function of the liver is to ensure the smooth flow of Qi. If qi is flowing smoothly your emotional state will be balanced too. If qi is blocked or obstructed then emotions such as anger, depression, frustration, feeling "wound up" will manifest.

If the qi is not flowing smoothly then physical symptoms can occur such as pain in the chest, feeling of a lump in the throat or distention of the abdomen. The liver is also linked to the health of the sinews and therefore has a direct impact on your flexibility and ability to move in a fluid way.

Experiments have shown that feelings of fear and anxiety reduce blood flow to the liver and thus impair its healthy function. This is in line with the TCM constructive cycle where the kidneys, associated with the emotion of fear, nourish the liver. Excessive fearfulness upsets the flow of energy from the kidneys to the liver.

An unhealthy liver can lead to muscle cramps, spasms, trembling and numbness, which all inhibit fluid movement.

Mentally, a healthy liver helps us to think ahead, to plan and organise so that we have a clear sense of direction, which obviously encourages the ability to move forward and flow. However, if it is out of balance then we can feel clouded and stuck.

Key guidelines for the health of your liver are to avoid highly fatty, deep fried, highly processed or denatured foods. Also, avoid alcohol, as the liver is responsible for metabolizing it. Reducing or removing alcohol from your diet can go a long way towards preserving your liver's energy and giving it a break.

Instead, make sure that celery, carrots, chard, broccoli, cabbage, asparagus, lemons, and black sesame seeds are included in your diet.

Peppermint tea and green tea are also good for the liver.

Here's a recipe that combines many of these foods to give your liver a helping hand. It's delicious too.

Since, green is the colour for the liver. Many dark green vegetables are great for supporting the liver and cooling liver heat.

Broccoli (or any dark green veg) with Garlic and Sesame Stir Fry Recipe
Prep time: 10 minutes
Cook time: 15 minutes
Serves 4

Ingredients
1 Tbsp. sesame seeds
1/2 cup chicken or vegetable stock
1 Tbsp. soy sauce
1 Tbsp. dark sesame oil
Vegetable oil
1 head broccoli florets, rinsed, patted dry, cut into bite-sized pieces
3 cloves of garlic, finely chopped

1. Toast the sesame seeds: Toast the sesame seeds by first sautéing in a pan on medium high heat. Cook until lightly browned and fragrant.
Put into a small bowl.

2. Mix stock, soy sauce, sesame oil: Mix the stock, soy sauce, and dark sesame oil together in a small bowl, set aside.

3. Par boil the broccoli in boiling water for 5 minutes tops, then drain.

4. Fry garlic: Heat the wok and add oil and garlic. Be careful not to burn
Then add the par boiled broccoli to the wok. Stir-fry for a couple of minutes.

5. Add the stock soy mixture and simmer: Add the stock, soy sauce and sesame oil mixture to the pan. Bring to a simmer. Reduce the heat and cover. Let cook for 2-3 minutes, until broccoli is still firm, but can be pierced with a fork. Remove from heat.

I like to treat recipes as a starting point. Have fun substituting different ingredients or adding your own twist to make these your own.

CHANGMING 3
Steamed Greens with Carrots and Tahini Miso Sauce

This is currently my number one favourite meal and it's great for your liver too.

The recipe is super quick and easy and once you've tried the Tahini (Sesame) and Miso sauce, you won't be able to get enough of it. The recipe below serves two adults and takes about five minutes to prepare and ten minutes to cook.

Ingredients:
Half a head of Broccoli
2/3 Carrots (organic if possible, they taste so much better)
Half a Green Cabbage
You can use any seasonal vegetables that are hanging around in your fridge.

Sauce:
2 tablespoons of Tahini (Light)
1 generous tablespoon of Brown Rice Miso
1 generous dollop of date syrup
1 dash of tamari
1 dash of toasted sesame oil
2 ladles of vegetable stock / water from the steamed veg

Method:
1. Wash and cut the carrots into large chunks
2. Place the carrots into the steamer and start steaming
3. Wash and cut the broccoli into chucky heads
4. Wash and dice the cabbage

5. Place the broccoli and cabbage into the steamer and add as another layer over the carrots. Steam for five minutes.

While the veg are steaming, make the sauce.

Tahini and Miso Sauce
1. Place 2 heaped tablespoons of Tahini in a pan with a very low heat.
2. Add 1 dollop of date syrup, toasted sesame oil and tamari soya sauce
3. Add 2 ladles of the steamed vegetable water and stir
4. Once the sauce has mixed well, turn off the heat and add 1 tablespoon of brown rice miso and continue to stir in well.

Place the steamed veggies in a bowl and generously dress with the hot sauce and serve.

You can also serve this with a portion of short grain brown rice.

The nutty flavour of the brown rice is delicious with this sauce.

Bon Appetite![12] ☺

---

[12] For more delicious recipes download *The Basic Chanming Cook Book* from Amazon for your kindle

SUMMARY

This section was all about finding your flow and learning to make life smooth. We explored the Daoist principles of accepting rather than resisting life, being like water and getting things done with effortless effort.

We introduced you to the flowing Silk Reeling exercise to promote fluidity in your movement. We guided you through the Daoist meditation technique of circulating your breath and energy through your Microcosmic Orbit to ignite the process of internal flow. We also shared a Dao Yoga or Kaimen exercise that is particularly good for supporting the energy of your liver.

We outlined the importance of having a fluid and flexible approach to your diet and then shared ways to look after your liver, the organ with responsibility for the flow of your blood and qi. We included a scrummy recipe that is delicious and supports your liver function.

We hope things are beginning to flow for you and we can progress to the next chapter where we consider Daoist approaches to getting what you want.

SECTION FOUR
Getting What You Want

This is a great chapter. It is all about getting what you want from life.

The Daoists see life as precious and so the ability to live a long life and enjoy it to its full is promoted as a worthy quest. We will introduce a number of ideas and practices for doing this and suggest you keep an open mind. Sometimes getting what you really want involves letting go of out-dated ideas and opening yourself to new possibilities.

We hope that by the end of this chapter you will have a different perspective on how to achieve your goals and that you will feel immediate benefits from the ideas and exercises we share with you.

CHAPTER 10
Three Daoist Principles

DAOIST PRINCIPLE 1
Softness Is the Strongest

In the West, we have a culture that overall idolises the yang (masculine traits) as superior to the yin (feminine traits). Being competitive, hard, arrogant or over confident tend to be promoted and the majority of leaders are expected to demonstrate such qualities if they are to earn respect.

We are trained from a young age and throughout the schooling system to be very yang with our thinking, our intentions and our actions. The messages we receive consciously and sub-consciously is that the person who shouts the loudest, runs the fastest, gets the best scores is to be admired and followed.

Winning as measured by external criteria takes priority over happiness, contentment and less easily measured activities like emotional intelligence and relationship building.

This yang intellectual mind is only interested in what it can see, touch, smell and hear. However, the subtle energy of the Dao is really the more powerful force. The invisible has little meaning, and is considered worthless and unreal to most people. Therefore, they only place importance on attitudes and activities that can manipulate this physical realm.

In fact, the title of this Chapter, "Getting what you Want", is too yang.

Often if you WANT something too much, it implies a neediness that is too emotional, and so the chapter should really be called:

"Surfing Life So You Have a High-Energy Experience and Attract What You Need", but that's a bit of a mouthful.

The flame that burns twice as bright burns half as long.
Laozi

Yin and Yang
The Daodejing talks of two kind of energies. The strong, aggressive kind that looks impressive is easy to flare up and is quick to burn out. Then there is the energy that appears weak and soft but is the most powerful conqueror.

Whilst the balance of yin and yang is a fundamental principle in Daoism, the yin is also revered as more powerful than the yang. The yin feminine gives birth to everything in this world. Mother earth nourishes and sustains us through life and it is to the earth that we return when we have exhausted our yang energy.

Our physical bodies are born from yin, nourished by yin and return to yin. There is no escape from this cycle. The yin is soft and yet it is the strongest. It achieves everything yet appears to do nothing. How can we learn from this and apply it to our own experience of life?

Being Yin

So what does it mean to develop your yin? Firstly we must bring our focus away from the yang activity of the mind and in to the yin sensing of the body. Away from the rational, logical, yes/no, right/wrong, black/white way of viewing the world and towards a more accepting holistic view of the world where the various qualities of different experiences are considered equally valid.

Be patient. Reacting to what is first presented is very yang. The yin way is to listen, to observe, to accept and to let things unfold naturally. Gently helping them along but not rushing to achieve a goal.

Learn to follow the energy of the situation rather than following what your brain thinks should happen. People describe following a gut feeling or a hunch. Being aware of this is the first step. Next is learning to follow this feeling at each step of the way rather than pushing for a particular result.

The female always surpasses the male with stillness. In her stillness, she is yielding.

Laozi

This is a practice that is about being fully present in the moment it allows you to sense and follow opportunities so the world opens for you in more ways than you can imagine.

If you learn to listen, the Dao will open to you and show you the way.

Becoming Softer
Your body is physical, it is condensed matter, it is solid, it is yang compared to your energy. Your energy is yin. In Lishi, we describe it as non-physical. It is invisible to the untrained eye and requires a greater level of sensitivity to feel its presence.

When practicing any art, if you focus on using physical force, then eventually it will create a practitioner that is hard, rigid and inflexible.

The first stage in developing your yin is to learn to soften your body. Yes, this involves relaxing your body but not how most people understand the word. Most people consider relaxing as being when you slump down in front of the telly. Daoists don't consider that relaxing, they call it dying.

In Daoism and in Lishi, relaxing occurs within a structured body. The structure is the yang within the yin. We must first learn the structure for our body and train it so that it can become a strong vessel for the yin. An unstructured, unconditioned body is like a mass of coiled and kinked hosepipes with stagnant water trapped, blocked and unable to flow.

We must learn to soften and relax our bodies whilst maintaining the aligned structure of all our body parts. In this way, our energy can flow throughout our body and we can begin to sense and develop this softer energy body. This is the start of becoming softer.

Softer Still

The body is the most visible tangible part of a person so it is a good starting point for our journey of self-discovery. It is a stepping-stone, to the deeper parts of who we are. The parts that we really intend to train and strengthen.

We condition the body as a vessel for our energy body so that we become more aware of the energetic part of who we are. This subtler, more refined experience allows us to become more sensitive to other changes we can make, on an even deeper level. We can start to recognise the effect that different emotions and thoughts have on our energy.

This greater sensitivity allows us to control and choose and cultivate the kinds of emotions and thoughts that make us better able to sense through our energy. Softening our thinking and calming our emotions increases our yin power. Bit by bit, the subtleties in the unseen inner worlds become real, tangible and workable. Then the next level of our training can begin as we continue to soften more.

Intention

So what does all of this have to do with getting what you want?

Patience young Padawan. We're getting to that.

Compared to your energy, your physical body is slow. Before you can move your arm, your energy has to be fired to make that movement possible. Your energy moves first then your physical body follows.

If you want to put your hand in your pocket to pay for your bag of brown rice from the health food shop you have to think the thought that fires the energy that moves the muscles that make your robot-like arm perform the required action.

Before you even got to the health food shop you were sat in your armchair at home, your mind visualised the goal you wanted to achieve (bag of brown rice in the cupboard). It set the intention and your energy followed the intention bringing your physical body along with you.

Intention plus action leads to the result you desire.

Some results, for example scratching an itchy nose, have a shorter timescale with fewer actions, require little energy and can be achieved relatively quickly.
Other results, for example writing this book, take longer, involve more activity requiring greater energy and a more relentless intention.

If all you want from life is to scratch an itch then you probably don't require a Daoist training. If however you are up for an adventure, learning to become more skilful with your energy is an endeavour well worth your while.

Pull, Don't Push
Once you have set an intention for what you want and are getting on with the necessary action to create it, it is important to monitor the frequency you are emitting. If your mind and energy are desperately grasping, craving your desired goal, if they are hard, yang, and pushing constantly towards it then it can actually slow your progress down.

If you are too hard in your attitude, if you want your goal too strongly it can be like the Bow Wave at the front of a battle ship. It sets up a pressure that energetically keeps your desired result just out of reach and the harder you push towards it the more it pushes it out of reach.

Knowing the manly, but clinging to the womanly, you become the valley of the world.

Laozi

If you focus too narrowly on your goal, it can lead to a blinkered view that considers only one way to achieve what you want. It blinds you to other opportunities that might get you there faster or might bring you even better results.

A yang approach like this, where your desire is so strong that it adds hardness, tensions, rigidity and a lack of flexibility, simply is not in keeping with the principles of Daoism we aim to embody.

The Daoist way is less yang. Of course, the need for a clear intention and relevant effortless effort is recognised but you should maintain your energy body in a state of open expectation. Allow the thing that you want to come to you

Cultivate thoughts and emotions with a true heart so your energy is attractive and vibrates at a level that harmonises with your desired outcome. Once you have set your intention, hold it lightly, let it go and have no emotional attachment to its achievement. Take action and do what needs to be done from that mental and emotional space.

Make Serendipity Your Friend

There is no single correct path to the things you want in life. Many roads lead to the same destination. The way someone tells you you should do something is just one way. The way you think you should do it is just one-way too.

The term serendipity was first coined in 1754 by Horace Walpole, in response to a Persian fairy-tale translated as The Three Princes of Serendip. It was derived from Serendip in the title, which is the Perso-Arabic name for Sri Lanka (Ceylon). The heroes of the story 'were always making discoveries, by accidents and sagacity, of things they were not in quest of'. This led to the definition of serendipity as the occurrence and development of events by chance in a happy or beneficial way.

This tale and the notion of serendipity is wonderfully Daoist in its approach. The life and career of a Daoist is similar to that of a butterfly who flits one way then another alighting on fragrant flowers by chance and at the behest of the prevailing winds.

This Daoist approach to life is increasingly being seen as highly desirable. Companies throughout the world are designing their workspaces to increase the likelihood of their employees making chance discoveries and accidents that lead to innovation.

The 2013 Wall Street Journal article The Science of Serendipity in the Workplace cites the design of the new google headquarters where a representative said, "We want it to be easy [for] Googlers to collaborate and bump into each other". This is just one example of the increasing importance being placed on serendipity as a positive force.[13]

---

[13]www.wsj.com/articles/SB100014241278873237981045784550812185 05870 (Have fun typing out that url! ☺)

You can't connect the dots looking forward; you can only connect them looking backward. So you have to trust that the dots will somehow connect in your future. You have to trust in something — your gut, destiny, life, karma, whatever. This approach has never let me down, and it has made all the difference in my life.

Steve Jobs

DAOIST PRINCIPLE 2
Timing

The Gongfu system we learn in Lishi is called Feng Shou or "Hand of the Wind". One of the skills that we work on is called timing. It is the ability to move at the correct moment and speed to harmonise with your partner and make a technique effective.

It doesn't matter how skilled you are in a technique, if you get the timing wrong, it will be ineffective. Understanding this on a physical, visceral level helps us to sense when the right time to act is. Not just in the training hall but in day-to-day life too.

The Roman philosopher Seneca once said that

"Luck Is What Happens When Preparation Meets Opportunity".

Being able to act at the right moment, being able to sense what to do and when is a skill that can be developed through preparation and practice.

Cherries
Rushing around like a headless chicken, striving for ill-considered goals whilst drenched in stress from an unbalanced lifestyle does not help you see, never mind seize opportunity when it comes to you.

Lightning seldom strikes twice, you can't take a second bite of the cherry and you never get a second chance to make a first impression.

If you equate Daoism purely with the hippyish notions of going with the flow then you are only realising part of the picture.

There is a time for being ahead,
a time for being behind;
a time for being in motion,
a time for being at rest;
a time for being vigorous,
a time for being exhausted;
a time for being safe,
a time for being in danger.

Laozi

Daoism is a practical philosophy and science that was developed as a way to lift its practitioners up to a better, more comfortable way of life. In many ways, Daoists were the first life coaches to walk the planet.

Making the most of opportunities and of the abundance of life is part and parcel of the Daoist lifestyle. Daoists don't subscribe to the idea of suffering so that they can get to heaven when they die. They align their thoughts and actions so that they can experience heaven or paradise on earth now.

They learn to be happy and content. They learn to see the little miracles that happen in their everyday lives. They learn not to want, because wanting is loaded with needy emotion.

Instead, they come from a place of balance and contentment and so attract more miracles into their lives.

Gongfu

In Lishi, we study Gongfu, which is the Chinese word that refers to any study, learning, or practice that requires patience, energy, and time to complete. In its original meaning, it can refer to any discipline or skill achieved through hard work and practice, not necessarily martial arts.

We also practise Qigong, which translates as Energy Work. The consistent element in the mastery of any of these arts is hard work through time. Gongfu is an art not just about fighting but also about an attitude to life. To be a master of whatever your thing is you need Gongfu.

If there are things, you want from life then you need to be prepared to study, to learn, to practise and to execute your skills impeccably when the time is right. If you develop this attitude and ability then when an opportunity collides with your preparation you will get results that will seem like magic or luck. Really, the appearance of overnight success will be because of the years of Gongfu and serendipity that allowed you to capitalise when the time is right.

Sense

It has been said that Lishi is one of the only true Yin-Yang Systems of Whole Body Cultivation in the world. The Daoist Arts of Lishi are divided into the Yin Arts and the Yang Arts.

Hand of the Wind Gong Fu is one section within the Yang Arts of Lishi. It is fast, dynamic and expressive. It trains your ability to affect the external world through the expression of your energy in particular ways.

We also practise the Yin Arts, which include exercises such as Kaimen Dao Yoga and Square Yard Taiji. These are slower, more inwardly focussed arts and they help develop energy awareness and sensitivity.

This is a crucial skill in getting what you want in life. The ability to listen with your energy so that you can feel your higher desires, feel when the time is right and when an opportunity is the right one is developed through practicing the yin arts.

Developing our abilities in both arts through our practise of Lishi, we learn when to be yin and when to be yang so we can achieve the best outcome and more easily get what we want.

The New York Times article "Cultivating the Art of Serendipity[14]" argues that, "At its birth, serendipity is a skill rather than a random stroke of good fortune." In other words, serendipity is something that people do. Following the ancient practise of Lishi, developing your abilities in both the yin arts and the yang arts, helps cultivate this skill so you can get what you want from life, and even better than that, in unexpected and magical ways.

---

[14]www.nytimes.com/2016/01/03/opinion/how-to-cultivate-the-art-of-serendipity.html

DAOIST PRINCIPLE 3
Don't Be Greedy, Don't Be Needy

As mentioned in a previous chapter, the celebrity culture and adverts that are pushed out by the media and big corporations constantly feed us the lie, that you or your life is not good enough. It doesn't matter what car you drive, you could buy a better, faster, shinier one. However, lovely your house looks it is always dated when compared to Living etc. Don't get me started on your clothes! You shabby, unstylish slob. They are so last season and you definitely need a complete makeover.

You don't. You look fine. They just want your energy in the form of money and attention. To get it they create fears that you are not good enough. Only then can they dangle their product in front of you as a means to regain the happiness you already felt before they invaded your world by interrupting your favourite TV show. Bastards!

By now, at this point in the book you probably realise that Daoism and navigating the craziness of life is full of dichotomies, paradox and balancing acts. Whilst experiencing heaven on earth, it is perfectly fine to get what you want but at the same time if you don't get it, that's fine too and you'll be just as happy either way.

We also have to walk the line between need and greed without wobbling too far either way.

There is a story of a famous yogi (although we cannot remember which one) who on his first visit to America was walking through the airport admiring the huge domed glass ceiling, the expanse of marble floors, the abundance of luxurious shops and the stern-faced, stressed-out people rushing from here to there. "They live in heaven" he said, "Yet they do not realise it."

If you compare the mental and emotional states of those airport travellers or any of the people, you see around you on your daily commute, if you compare them with the laughing smiling faces of children in developing countries who have practically nothing and yet feel immense joy and happiness simply from the gift of life, who is richer?

Those Damn Virtues Again

In earlier chapters, we discussed the Daoist virtues of humility and frugality. Humility is about minimising your ego. Frugality is about minimising wasted energy (which money is a form of). They are about becoming softer and more yin about your wants and intentions. They are not about being excessive in your desires nor are they about feelings of neediness.

They are about nourishing, nurturing, and cultivating goodness in the moment. Following your bliss rather than striving for big goals.

Learn to accept and appreciate the abundance of life and just how fortunate you are to have been born where you were born, to live where you live, to have the opportunities you have as well as the material wealth that surrounds you.

You Have All That You Need

Try this right now. In this very moment what do you want and need?

We don't mean tonight or tomorrow or next week or something, that would be 'nice' to have.

Right now, is everything good? You pretty much have everything for your immediate happiness and contentment in this moment.

You are comfortable, warm, full, relaxed, happy, reading an awesome book[15] and doing what you want to be doing.

Even if that isn't 100% true, we bet it could be true for you very quickly and easily if you put the kettle on, wrapped a blanket around you and had a little nibble.

Life is good my friend. Now how do we make it gooder?

From a place of things being just fine, what would make things 5% better than they are?

5% is nothing really. Anyone could make his or her life 5% better and yet it's also a step in the right direction. A meaningful improvement. Enjoy a few minutes thought on what would make life 5% better and get excited about how easy that would be to make happen.

When you've done that, consider what 50% better would look like. If things were an additional half as good as they are now how would that be? What would bring your experience of life to that level? What would have to happen? How might that occur for you in serendipitous ways or in straightforward actions that you can take?

Cool huh?

First thing is always to be grateful for all that's good in your life. If you can't be happy and satisfied in this moment, you won't be happy and satisfied when you get to 5%, 50% or 100% better.

Some people say that life is about the journey and not the destination. We say it can be about more than just the journey. Enjoy now. Enjoy the journey. Enjoy the destination.

---

[15] If you agree then a positive review on amazon would be a lovely way of saying "thank you" ☺

Nervous Wreck

Our autonomic nervous system (ANS) takes care of our bodily functions without us having to think about it. Breathing, heartbeat, digestion are some of the unconscious tasks that our body just gets on with thanks to the ANS. It has two primary branches, the sympathetic and the parasympathetic.

The parasympathetic nervous system (PNS) controls homeostasis and the body at rest and is responsible for the body's "rest and digest" function.

The sympathetic nervous system (SNS) controls the body's responses to a perceived threat and is responsible for the "fight or flight" response or in a modern context, to train, play hard, work hard - to perform at high levels of intensity.

You can think of our sympathetic nervous system as our accelerator. It ignites the energy and focus. The parasympathetic branch is our brake. It pulls the sympathetic branch back into a 'rest and digest' state so we can restore our energy and perform again tomorrow.

Many modern goal setting and motivational speakers try to tap in to the sympathetic nervous systems fight or flight response as a way to flood your body with adrenaline, pump you up and get you to take action.

Whilst that can be effective in the short-term, as a long-term strategy it is neither sustainable nor healthy.

In Daoist practise, the use of the sympathetic nervous system to motivate you should be eradicated. Maintaining the body in a state of relaxation where you are nourishing your body is of primary importance.

According to Paul King[16], our resilience and capacity to be at our best under pressure can be supported by being open in our posture, increasing our sense of length, softening the front of our body (a gentle smile helps), and working with the breath to bring our autonomic nervous system into balance.

These are all regular practises within Lishi. You can also help your body to stay in this ideal state whilst working towards and obtaining your goals by learning to live simpler and discovering that you don't lack in any way but actually already have a rich lifestyle.

Changing your priorities so that your health and spiritual development is more important than egotistical success or material gain will transform your experience of life. Design a life where your wants and needs are easily met.

Learn to be happy with what you have. Find joy in your training, practise and development. The journey will unfold as it should and opportunities will come when you are ready. No need to rush. No need to hurry. Enjoy now.

---

[16] (Source: SOMATIC INTELLIGENCE: WORKING WITH AND THROUGH THE BODY. Coaching Perspectives – The Association for Coaching Global Magazine, October 2016 – Issue 11)

We think if we work harder and achieve some goal, then we'll be happier. However, the research is clear that every time you've a success, your brain changes what success means. So for you, if happiness is on the opposite side of success, you'll never get there. But if you increase your levels of happiness in the midst of a challenge, what we find is that all of your success rates rise dramatically.

Shawn Achor

CHAPTER 11
Three Lishi Exercises

EXERCISE 1
Standing Qigong

This exercise is similar to the previous qigong exercise we covered in Chapter Two but with different arm positions. In this version, you stand with your arms out to the side at shoulder height. It trains you to open your body and your energy centres to receive.

Either you can do this in bear stance, which is where you stand with your feet parallel, hip width apart and toes pointing forward or you can do it in horse stance. In horse stance, you take your feet wider than shoulder width apart and bend your knees until you can feel your muscles are working.

Whichever stance you choose, always start by rooting in to the 9 points of contact on each foot then bringing your breath into the lower section and dropping your awareness to your Dantian.

Hold this stance stable as you raise your arms upwards at the side of your body so that the palms are turned up and held at shoulder height as far to the side of you as possible.

Use your abdominal muscles to gently tuck your pelvis under, lengthen your spine up to the crown of the head and slightly lift and open the chest and shoulders.

Look down the bridge of your nose towards your Dantian and gently close your eyes until there is just a slit of light. You shouldn't be able to see anything but you shouldn't be in complete darkness.

Keep the breath relaxed and slow into that lower section and hold the position for as long as you can. Aim for 30 seconds to start with and then over the days and weeks aim to increase to a minute then 2 minutes and so on. Some Masters will stand for hours but we don't suggest trying that just yet.

As you stand and maintain the posture, keep 9 points of contact firmly rooted, your breath slow and deep, your awareness in your Dantian and your chest, shoulders and palms open. If any tension creeps in, simply relax it. The more you practise this, the faster your body will become conditioned.

As your body becomes stronger, the feelings of tension will disperse and you will feel your body opening and filling with energy. Before long, what starts as an agonising torture is transformed into an energising event that you find yourself looking forward to every day.

Not everyone will make it that far but those that do, will reap the rewards.

EXERCISE 2
Abundance Kaimen

If you've done the standing qigong, you might like the idea of having a little sit down. In this Dao Yoga Kaimen exercise, you will sit on the floor with an upright posture, your legs and feet together and extended in front of you. This is called Double Plough Stance. Place the hands comfortably on the floor either side of you.

As with all Kaimen, the exercise is split into two sections, the sequence and the extension. During the sequence, keep the movements as relaxed as possible and harmonise each movement with an in-breathe or an out breathe.

On the extension aim to move further extending your range of movement whilst keeping the body soft and relaxed and breathing naturally.

SEQUENCE
1. Breathe IN as you raise the hands making a cup formation by placing the little finger edge of your hands together in front of your belly.

2. Breathe OUT as you maintain the hand formation and turn your shoulders to the left. Keep the hands in front of your belly and your chin over your sternum.

3. Breathe IN as you maintain the hand formation and turn back to face forwards.

4. Breathe OUT as you maintain the hand formation and turn your shoulders to the right. Keep the hands in front of your belly and your chin over your sternum.

5. Breathe IN as you maintain the hand formation and turn back to face forwards.

6. Breathe OUT as you place the hands back on the floor.

REPEAT 1 – 6 but turning to the right first and then the left.

REPEAT the sequence again on both sides.

EXTENSON
Repeat the sequence, but as you turn the torso do so as far as you comfortably can and then extend the arms still in the cup formation as far round as you can. You can turn the head to look behind you. Don't hold the position. Keep the movement relaxed and breathe in and out, as you need.

REPEAT Extension

EXERCISE 3
Inner Smile

Daoist practise involves internal practise (Neidan inner alchemy) as well as the external exercises. We are now going to create positive energy in each of your major organs. You know the ones that work tirelessly all day and night without giving them a second thought or ever saying "Thank you" to them.

This is a simple guided process where you look within, smile and create feelings of love and gratitude in each of these organs.

1. Sit cross-legged on the floor (or if you can't do that, use a straight-backed chair. Hold your spine upright just as we showed you in the vertical planking exercise earlier. Allow the muscles of your neck, shoulders, throat, chest, back and abs to feel relaxed.
2. Place your tongue on the roof of your mouth and take a few relaxed breaths into your lower section. Clear your mind so your focus is with the breath. Look down the bridge of the nose and lightly close your eyes until there is just a slit of light.
3. Allow your face to relax into a gentle, natural smile and notice how this feeling spreads through your body.
4. Bring your attention to your Dantian, an energy reservoir just below and behind your belly-button and feel your energy gathering at that point as you continue breathing and smiling gently into your Dantian as the energy builds.
5. When you are ready, lift this energy to your heart. Infuse your inner smile with the colour red as you send love and kindness to your heart. Thank it for everything it does for you. Feel it opening and responding to this attention. Feel

it smiling back at you and becoming stronger and more energised.

6. When you are ready, move your attention to your lungs. Take deeper, fuller breathes and see them expanding with a bright white light. Feel them fully inflate; feel their power as you send them feelings of courage and honesty. Thank them for filling you with the power of the universe and fuelling your whole body from moment to moment. Feel them swell and respond to this attention. Feel your lungs projecting the white light of truth back at you as they become stronger and more energised.

7. When you are ready, move this energy to your liver (just below your right lung). Infuse your inner smile with the colour of a vibrant green forest as you send forgiveness and generosity to your liver. Feel gratitude for the liver's work in detoxifying the body. Feel the liver emitting the cool restful energy of an oak tree as it becomes smoother, shinier and more relaxed.

8. When you are ready, move this energy to your kidneys, either side of your spine towards your lower back. Infuse your inner smile with the colour bluey black as you send kind and gentle energy to your kidneys. Thank them for everything it does for you. Feel it opening and responding to this attention. Feel it smiling back at you and becoming stronger and more energised.

9. When you are ready, move this energy to your stomach. Infuse your inner smile with a bright yellow as you send a centring energy of fairness and compassion to your stomach. Thank it for digesting your food and restoring energy in your body. Feel it relaxing and responding to this attention as any anxiety melts away under the compassionate gaze of this bright yellow smile. Feel it smiling back at you and becoming more relaxed and effective.

10. Next, send the smiling energy down into the urinary bladder, urethra, genitals, and perineum.

Women: The collection point for female sexual energy is located about three inches below the navel, midway between the ovaries. Smile the accumulated energies into the ovaries, uterus, and vagina. Thank the ovaries for making hormones and giving you sexual energy. Bring the combined sexual, smiling, and virtue energies up to the navel, and visualize the energies spiralling into that point.

Men: The collection point for male sexual energy is located one-and-a-half inches above the base of the penis in the area of the prostate gland and seminal vesicles. Smile, and visualize the accumulated energies spiralling down into the prostate gland and testicles. Thank them for making hormones and giving you sexual energy. Bring the combined sexual, smiling, and virtue energies up to the navel, and spiral them into that point.

11. Allow the warmth and energy of all of your organs to continue smiling at each other nourishing your internal. Any excess energy can collect back in your Dantian where you can store it. When you are ready, gently open your eyes. Cover the eyes with the heels of your hand and take six deep breathes in through the nose and out through the nose.

Acclimatise yourself with the surrounding environment then gently get up and carry on with your day taking the wonderful feelings with you.

CHAPTER 12
Three Changming Lifestyle Recommendations

CHANGMING 1
Do Something Purely For the Joy of Doing It

There is a difference between knowledge and understanding and wisdom. Reading about these principles will give you an awareness but in order to understand you have to put that knowledge into practise. You have to do.

Many beginners who come to our classes think that they understand after they have done something once or twice.

"Got it. What's next?"

No, no. no. You don't have it at all. It is not until you have done something a thousand times that you start to understand. To develop true wisdom will take 10,000 times.

This was the magic number of practise hours that Malcolm Gladwell suggests in his book *Outliers,* was the minimum requirement for people considered geniuses in their field.

A helpful saying to keep things real is "To know and not to do, is not to know".

In Daoism, we are not practising in order to get somewhere or achieve something in particular. It is not goal driven.

We practise because it is in the repetition that you gain knowledge, then understanding and then wisdom. There is joy in repetition and so we practise for the pleasure and nourishment that we feel from doing our practise.

As we spend time working on our craft in this way, we discover mastery, not as a goal we are striving for but as a quality that we embody. So, pick something that you love to do purely for the joy of doing it. It might be one of the exercises from Lishi; it might be walking in nature or having a catch up with friends over a cup of green tea.

Go do it or at least schedule a time when you will. Have no objective. Don't even *try* to enjoy it or focus on anything in particular nor steer things in any particular way. Just be.

Start bringing this feeling and attitude to other things that you do. Expand it so that your whole life is lived in a state of joy about whatever it is you find yourself doing. Use it as a compass so that you do less of the things that you don't enjoy and spend more time doing things you do.

Pleasure is always derived from something outside you, whereas joy arises from within.

Eckhart Tolle

CHANGMING 2
Gratitude Journal

It can be very easy to forget how blessed and lucky we are. There are a multitude of things we can pay attention to each day. Unless we make it a conscious habit to remind ourselves of the miracles that happen to us regularly, we can quickly lose sight of this truth.

Creating a daily routine of reminding yourself how lucky you are will expand your awareness and actually increase your luck.

Richard J. Wiseman, author of *The Luck Factor* and Professor of the Public Understanding of Psychology at the University of Hertfordshire spent over ten years researching how you can make yourself luckier. He discovered that lucky people generate good fortune via four basic principles.

They:
- are skilled at creating and noticing chance opportunities,
- make lucky decisions by listening to their intuition,
- create self-fulfilling prophesies via positive expectations and
- adopt a resilient attitude that transforms bad luck into good.

To help develop your ability to get lucky, write a journal each day, or at a minimum each week. Use the journal as a tool to help place your awareness on all of the good bits of your life, the serendipitous events, and the positive lessons learned. This will soften you to the fluffiness of life, help you make connections between seemingly unrelated events, increase your ability to spot and benefit from opportunities and generally expand your luck.

When you are in a state of gratitude, your energy is lifted and you make better decisions.

Another practise you could try is to write on a slip of paper one thing per day that you feel grateful for or pleased about, then fold it and put it in a jar. Once a month or quarter or year throw a review party for yourself where you open up the jar and read over all the great things you've noticed and been grateful for.

If the above suggestions don't give you enough ideas to write in your journal, then write something you are grateful about for each of the following:

- Something about your body
- Something about a personal quality you have
- Something about a person you encountered today
- Something about your environment
- Something about being alive

Try it for 3 days and see what difference it makes. Another 3 days. Then another. Before you can say, "Life is good" you'll be well on your way to having everything you need.

CHANGMING 3
Prime Time

When people say, "he was in his prime" they are referring to the state or time of greatest vigour or success in a person's life.

Daoists rise and do their practise in the temple during the early hours of the morning when the air is uncluttered by the activity of the masses. It is prime time for their practise. It is also prime time for yours.

When you wake rather than it being in response to the sharp call of your alarm followed by a hurried rush to get to work. Aim to start your day in a more yin way. Create a routine that is a gradual and gentle slide from rest into activity.

If you are waking up before sunrise then we recommend getting a light alarm clock. They have a number of benefits over their noisy equivalents. These include boosting healthy cortisol levels, balancing melatonin and helping if you have a propensity towards Seasonal Affective Disorder or Depression.

To continue your gentle wake up, sit up in bed and reach for your gratitude journal. Read over last night's entry and really feel grateful again for all of those things. Add at least 3 more things that you feel (or could feel) grateful for.

This should take no longer than 3-5 minutes and will put you in a much better mood than most people at this time of the morning.

Get out of bed and do the Lishi warmup. Gentle moves that get your circulation going, warm the major muscles and joints of the body[17].

---

[17] If you would like a video to talk you through this, please check out our High Energy Tai Chi course on Udemy.com

Whilst you're warming your body up you can also warm your mind up by just saying nice stuff to yourself. Things like "Wow! I'm amazing! It's so cool that I am looking after my body and programming my mind like this. This is cool. My body is getting more and more flexible every day. I feel great. People comment on how happy I am. I see opportunities all around me and I choose which ones to take and when. I'm developing myself all the time. I am so lucky to have tapped in to this ancient wisdom. Life is getting better all the time. I'm so excited about the positive serendipitous events that will occur for me today."

They're just some ideas. You can develop your own positive dialogue with yourself. Talk to yourself as if you're talking to your best friend. After all, if you're not your best friend, who is?

Once you've given yourself a good talking to and warmed up your body. You can do the one Direction Breathing Exercise from Chapter 3. As you breathe out, push your hands forwards and send your energy out into the day ahead as a positive light. See the things that you are doing today going well.

See everything unfolding nicely and see you being the way that you want to be. If you have some big goals or projects that you are working on at the moment, pump some positive vibes their way too and see them in their completed state. See them as done.

Then let go of any attachment to your day or your goals and agree to accept things as you find them.

Spend a moment in silent contemplation, perhaps doing one of the standing Qigong exercises we've shared with you. Remind yourself of the virtues that you want to embody today.

Remember that the virtues are something you practise and that by practising them you become them. Embody those feelings now whilst the world is quiet and calm.

Let them become your centre that you can return to throughout the day if you feel yourself pulled or pushed off balance. Then when you are ready, bring the session to a close and move on to whatever comes next in your day.

What we've outlined is just a method. It is a training. You won't necessarily have to do this every day for the rest of your life. One day you will just wake up and be in an optimum, grateful, enlightened state but who knows when that day will be. Until then, this methodology will help you.

SUMMARY

So do you have what you wanted from this section?

We covered the Daoist approach to getting things, which may well be different from what you expected, but hopefully you get the benefits of becoming softer in your approach to your goals so that you can take advantage of the serendipity of life. Instead of a headlong charge, enjoy the dance of life as you move towards your desired lifestyle.

We considered the role of timing and of being ready when opportunities present themselves and we did some exercises that help open your body to accept and receive.

Finally, we outlined three Changming guidelines for cultivating a gratitude attitude, setting your days up so you start in the right place to live fearlessly and simply enjoy life to the max.

If you put all of this into practise you will already be starting to get the hang of being happy which is the topic of the next section.

SECTION FIVE
Being Fearless

In this section, we will explore the Daoist concept of living a fearless life. Many of the students who walk through the doors of our classes have either told us or shown us that they suffer from anxiety, nervousness, low self-esteem or a lack of confidence.

All of these things are just different ways of saying "I'm scared!" or "Life scares me". They are not the only ones.

Much of the conflict and turmoil of the world comes from the fact that people are frightened, stressed and unhappy. Learning to take control of this part of your experience no matter what is happening in your life is an integral part of being a powerful spiritual warrior.

By the end of the chapter, you will think of fearlessness in a different way and have a few options for how you can start to live a fearless life.

CHAPTER THIRTEEN
Three Daoist Principles

PRINCIPLE 1
The Daoist Virtues
and Your Personal Values

We live in a universe of cause and effect. Everything is connected and inter-related and the smallest of actions in one place can have consequences on the other side of the planet. Equally, the internal states that we consider important will drive our thoughts and behaviours and affect our experience of life.

In Daoist thought, cause and effect are simultaneous and instantaneous. As human beings, our thoughts and actions are energy projections. If we are fearful, we project that into the world, we notice all the scary things and dwell in feelings of fear. We are the initiator of self-fulfilling prophecies that reinforce our feelings and keep us trapped in a space of weakness instead of power.

There are a number of different reasons for why we might conclude that the world is a scary place. The first we will explore are your own personal set of values.

If we value achievement, winning and having money then these values will cause us to think in ways that have consequences for the direction of our lives and our energy will reflect those intentions.

If we value friendships, love and generosity then these values will likely lead to different actions and different results and our energy will be attuned to that way of being.

Often our values are shaped when we are young, influenced by our parents, teachers and friends. They form unconsciously based on our life experiences and the examples set by the people around us.

At any time in life though we can choose to evaluate these personal values, redefine them and cultivate new ones through the way that we think and act. We must learn to shed those values that have been draped upon us by others and instead look inwards to discover what is most important to us, what we value and what energy we most want to imbue.

At its core, most of the fears and anxiety we feel can be traced back to a single concern. The concern that we are not good enough.

This is a survival fear based on whether our tribe would consider us "enough" and therefore whether we would be "in" or "out".

However, in today's world, where does the criteria for deciding whether you are enough come from? Babies are not born with low self-esteem, they don't feel insecure, lack confidence or fear whether they are enough. These are all things that we learn.

The Dao doesn't set the criteria for whether you are worthy or not. You passed that test when the first of your Dads swimmers plunged into the soft comfort of your Mothers egg. You already beat over a billion others and won the prize of this thing called life.

That achievement dwarfs everything else you have done and everything else you will ever do. You made it. You are a success. You are enough and you won the greatest prize on offer in this universe.

Instead of focussing on the criteria for success or failure that you learned from your family, your school, your employer or society in general, focus instead on the success of making it this far.

Instead of trying to beat others or be something other than who you are in order to be accepted or feel like you are worthy, focus your attention on cultivating the virtues and your fears will drop away.

This is a first step towards discovering and refining your essence.

Value the Virtues
As mentioned earlier, Daoists over the millennia have developed a set of values that they call virtues. These virtues are ways of being and principles for living that guide their mental focus and daily actions. They are something that they practise and cultivate in order to embody and express these virtues.

There are many Daoist virtues but the ones that they all agree on are known as the three treasures. In the Daodejing, Laozi describes them thus:

"Here are my three treasures. Guard and keep them!

The first is compassion;

The second, frugality;

The third, refusal to be 'foremost of all things under heaven'.

For only he that has empathy is truly able to be fearless; only he that is frugal is able to be generous. Only he that refuses to be foremost of all things is truly able to become chief of all Ministers."

So there you have them. Compassion, frugality and refusal to be 'foremost of all things under heaven', what we understand to be humility.

Contentment
These three treasures are to be cultivated for the positive effect that they have on the life of a practitioner of Daoism as well as the effect they have on others. They are practises that if everyone chose to cultivate would have beneficial impacts on our interpersonal relationships, the harmony of our society and the balance and survival of our environment and ecosystems.

Placing these virtues as the guiding lights for your behaviour will bring you to a place of contented fearlessness. Of course, you don't have to live your life this way. You are free to experiment with any combination of values and discover what your unique combination generates.

However, if millions of wise old dudes and dudesses throughout time have experimented with different ways of living and have agreed that these three treasures are the bees' knees, we'd probably say they are worth listening to and worth taking for a spin around the block.

Compassion
This is about recognising that life can be tough at times and that people do suffer. Being aware of this, we do our best to avoid acting in ways that make life more difficult for others. Through our deeds we consider whether there will be harmful consequences for others and therefore do what we can to avoid causing harm.

However, the first person to practise being compassionate towards is yourself. You must heal and forgive yourself for any hardships you have suffered and for any harm, you might have caused in the past.

Self-flagellation, beating yourself up mentally or wallowing in self-pity are not part of the Daoist way. Free yourself from these negative practises by cultivating compassion for who you are and your journey so far.

Practising compassion for yourself is a process of accepting yourself for who you are. Accepting your strengths and your successes as well as your near misses and foul shots. Accepting them as perfect in every way. Uniquely beautiful, worthy and enough.

Until you have healed and strengthened, your own mind, body and spirit there is a limit to what you can do for others. Avoid harming others but do not rush to become other people's saviours. Have compassion for others journeys but understand that their journey is part of their Dao, it is the lessons that they must learn in order to heal themselves and become strong.

Nobody else can do it for them. Others can show them how, by the example they set. Have empathy for others suffering but do not let that affect you emotionally. Being an example of compassionate strength is more helpful than being a sobbing emotional wreck.

All of the Daoists we have met from all over the world are very strong individuals. They are not emotional nor evangelical. They care and they support where they can but their compassion does not weaken nor deter them from their own path.

Humility

Refusal to be 'foremost of all things under heaven'. We love this because it runs counter to the messages that the media and our society promote. To be the best, to be a success, to be a winner; surely, those are the things to strive for and that will make you happy. No, those things actually take you away from happiness and contentment.

Once you have won, where to next? When you have made it to the top, there is only one direction to go unless you spend the rest of your days fending off others trying to topple you from your throne. Happiness and contentment is not to be found at the top. Success is a prize for the ego.

Fear is a trait of the ego too. Our natural state is one of loving kindness. When you learn how to lose the fear and live your true nature, you will have nothing to lose and your actions will come from a place of generosity because you have more than enough. You are more than enough.

There is a great country you need to conquer before you set out to conquer the world

Chinese proverb

Refusing to be foremost is where contentment can be found because most of our fears are wrapped up in our desire to be foremost and therefore to be seen as worthy. Worthy of praise, worthy of money, worthy of love. It's complete bullshit. Drop it.

Have you ever lay on your back and looked up at the stars on a dark evening? It is hard not to be in awe of the vastness of life.

When you recognise just how tiny we actually are, what an inconsequential speck of dust you are in this huge whirling cosmos, you open a doorway that leads from self-importance towards a humble happiness.

We are all inconsequential specks in this huge swirling universe but somehow we are here so we might as well enjoy the ride.
Remember, humility is not about telling people how rubbish you are, what a loser you are, or in any way under-playing your unique qualities, that is a false humility.

Humility is about accepting everything about yourself, your talents and your weaknesses, enjoying them for what they are, chuckling about them, changing them if you like but not striving to be better than others.

Frugality
Although the world is abundant, there is no reason to be wasteful. Excessive material possessions require time, energy and money to maintain and store. Resources that would be better spent on cultivating the Dao and living in a space of happiness and contentment.

Instead, the virtue of frugality encourages us to live a lifestyle of simplicity where our wants and needs are modest and neither our time, energy nor money is being drained by our life set up.

Let's be clear. Frugality is not the same as poverty. There are many things to be enjoyed in life. It is nice to have a comfortable home with a big TV where you can watch your favourite box set when you fancy it. Frugality is about finding the right balance.

Look for those things in your life that are a drain and shed them. Release them. Let them go. Create space for doing nothing, for enjoying simple pleasures and for activities that strengthen and energise you.

You might encounter resistance to doing this. Either in the form of internal conflict and arguments for clinging to old ideas of what is important or in the form of judgement and concern from well-meaning friends and family who are of a different mind-set.

Learning to dissolve these conflicts and resistance is a good training.

Letting go of the trappings of "success" or even letting go of those actions and habits that are approved indicators that you're a successful person takes courage and is part of the alchemy of becoming fearless.

Trying Them On
Sometimes people confuse fearlessness with confidence, courage or bravery. They are not the same thing. Confidence, courage and bravery suggest a need to do, be or have something. Fearlessness is simply a complete absence of fear.

When you have no fear, you just act in accordance with your environment and your inner nature.

Fear simply doesn't exist for you and so you don't need confidence, courage or bravery in order to act. There is no need to pump yourself up or build a particular feeling in order to get you to act.
The complete absence of fear leaves you free to behave one-hundred percent naturally with no inner judgement about what you do.

To be fearless is to be free and to be free is one of the cornerstones of Daoist practise.

As with everything, there is a dichotomy. You cannot be free until you have experienced what it is to be shackled. If you have felt restricted or trapped by fears then be grateful that they are now pointing the way to complete freedom.

Considering the Daoist virtues of compassion, humility and frugality against your own personal values, how well aligned are they?

Do the three treasures sound good to you?
Would they enrich your life?

If so, ponder the ways that you could make them part of how you live each day.

Look for little shifts you can make in your thinking and actions and notice the challenges and opportunities that come from this.

It's unlikely it will be an overnight transformation but little by little, you can start to align yourself with a way of being that has been proven for thousands of years to bring happiness and contentment to the lives of millions. Worth a shot, don't you say?

PRINCIPLE 2
Become an Eternal Child

It is tempting to think that who we are is who we are and that will never change. As Harvard Psychologist Dan Gilbert[18] puts it, "Human beings are works in progress that mistakenly think they're finished." We somehow imagine that the person we are right now is the person we'll be for the rest of time but in reality that just isn't true.

His research has shown that on a number of different measures, our perception of how much we will change in the next ten years is much smaller than the amount we consider we have changed in the last ten years.

The Daoists recognised this and codified different stages that we go through in life including how our energy changes as we progress through each stage from birth and towards death.

Recognising these natural changes and holding life as the most precious gift, they developed practises that promote longevity. The longer you live, the more you get to enjoy the precious gift of life and the more time you have to train and develop your energy and become an immortal.

If you read the old texts of Laozi, Zhaungzi or the Eight Immortals it might strike you that these Daoist sages seem extremely child-like. They are playful, innocent, free-roaming rascally sorts who delight in telling stories, wandering aimlessly through mountains and valleys, playing hide-and-seek with the village children, enjoying a cup of tea or a jug of wine, and all variety of other simple pleasures.

---

[18]www.ted.com/talks/dan_gilbert_you_are_always_changing

Despite their number of years and their wisdom, they maintain the qualities of a young energy and don't seem weighed down by the responsibilities of life. In essence, they are fearless and free.

We don't stop playing because we grow old; we get old because we stop playing

George Bernard Shaw

In our rush to adulthood, we are sometimes keen to shed the traits of childhood and adopt a demeanour of seriousness so we are taken more seriously. Being considered "grown up" rather than "childish" are traits that are often encouraged and rewarded.

Seriousness is grave and this links back to the old Roman word *Gravis* meaning heavy and its obvious links with gravity. In other words, being serious is a heavy burden that weighs you down.

To avoid being weighed down by life avoid being serious and instead cultivate child-like qualities.

Let Go
Babies and young children live more fully in each moment. They don't hold on to emotions but experience them fully then move on to the next.

We've all seen a small child or baby flip from tears to hysterical laughter in an instant. This willingness to let go is a key component of resilience that is good to cultivate.

Be Divergent

A kids understanding of the world is not fully formed and so the possibilities of life are endless. This promotes a sense of awe and wonder, which aids divergent thinking and is seen as an essential capacity for creativity. It involves being able to see multiple approaches to a problem and multiple answers to a question.

Creativity expert Sir Ken Robinson gives the example of the question "How many uses can you think of for a paper clip?"

While most people might think of up to 15 or so answers, a 'divergent thinker' could come up with a couple hundred more. A longitudinal study gave a test of divergent thinking for which reaching above a certain score indicated 'genius' status in this type of thinking.

98% of the kindergarten children who took the test scored at genius level but as they grew older, the study found that those same students' divergent thinking scores declined[19].

No baby is born fearful. Fears are taught and they are learned. Other members our tribe teach us, shape us and control our behaviours by creating fears and manipulating them.

If you shed these fears, if you can no longer be manipulated and controlled in this way you can hang on to your divergent ways of thinking.

---

[19] Source, Ken Robinsons TED Talk – Do schools kill creativity?

Rather than making you more at risk and therefore being something to fear, being divergent will enhance your creativity, increase your chances of survival and expressing yourself creatively and therefore break the self-fulfilling prophesies of a fear-filled life.

The fears we are all taught create a matrix that limits our ability to express ourselves fully but worse than that, it teaches us to reinforce those fears and teach them to others.

When limits are placed on what is acceptable and what is possible, our ability to be creative shrinks.

Be childlike, be divergent and keep your creative genius alive.

Simple Contentment
Children can find happiness and joy in the simplest of things. It's a common lament of parents that their child has more fun with the wrapping paper or a box that an expensive toy came in than in the actual toy itself.
This ability to find joy in the simplest of things is a wonderful ability. One that wards off depression, mental illness and other faulty ways of thinking. To a child, the world is an awesome, amazing place. As you grow up that does not change. The world is still an awesome amazing place. If you don't see and feel that anymore, it is because you have changed. Time to turn back the clocks on that one.

How good are you at getting scared? At working yourself up into a nervous frenzy? At blowing your fears up to epic proportions?

Wouldn't it be preferable if you improved your ability to just drop all of that, just be and just tap in to your child-like nature that gets excited and happy about the possibilities and simple things in life?

Go on then.

Society is Bananas

An urban fable tells of an experimenter who put five monkeys in a large cage. High up at the top of the cage, well beyond the reach of the monkeys, is a bunch of bananas. Underneath the bananas is a ladder.

The monkeys immediately spot the bananas and one begins to climb the ladder. As he does, however, the experimenter sprays him with a stream of cold water.

Then, he proceeds to spray each of the other monkeys. The monkey on the ladder scrambles off, and all 5 sit for a time on the floor, wet, cold, and bewildered. Soon, though, the temptation of the bananas is too great, and another monkey begins to climb the ladder. Again, the experimenter sprays the ambitious monkey with cold water and all the other monkeys as well.

When a third monkey tries to climb the ladder, the other monkeys, wanting to avoid the cold spray, pull him off the ladder and beat him.

Now one monkey is removed and a new monkey is introduced to the cage. Spotting the bananas, he naively begins to climb the ladder. The other monkeys pull him off and beat him.

Here's where it gets interesting. The experimenter removes a second one of the original monkeys from the cage and replaces him with a new monkey. Again, the new monkey begins to climb the ladder and, again, the other monkeys pull him off and beat him - *including the monkey who had never been sprayed*.

By the end of the experiment, none of the original monkeys were left and yet, despite none of them ever experiencing the cold, wet, spray, they had all learned never to try to go for the bananas.

Grow Up

If you can be playful as an adult, it will lift you up and raise your spirits. Other people who you meet will be inspired and lifted up too.

The most charismatic people in life have a twinkle in their eye, a cheeky smile and a playfulness about their approach even to the most serious of issues.

Their ability to be fearless and lead by keeping emotions light is part of what makes people want to be around them and be led by them.

Be content with what you have;
rejoice in the way things are.
When you realize there is nothing lacking,
the whole world belongs to you

Laozi

Surely, it is more mature to adopt an attitude that has these positive effects on your well-being and the experience of people around you.

Being serious should not be worn like a badge or a shield that denotes intelligence or wisdom. It is far wiser and intelligent to bring a lighter energy to grave circumstances where a solution is called for.

Time to ponder all the ways that you could bring more playtime into your life. Consider whether you spend enough time doing the things you enjoy or maybe whether you spend enough time enjoying the things that you do.

If you were completely fearless, what would you change?

What would you do?

How would you be?

PRINCIPLE 3
Heaven on Earth

Happiness is just one of many emotions. According to Wikipedia (who definitely knows her stuff), "an emotion is any relatively brief conscious experience characterized by intense mental activity and a high degree of pleasure or displeasure". She also says that the scientific discourse has drifted to other meanings and there is no consensus on a definition.

According to some theories, emotions are states of feeling that result in physical and psychological changes that influence our behaviour. The physiology of emotion is closely linked to arousal of the nervous system with various states and strengths of arousal relating, apparently, to particular emotions. In other words, we're still trying to figure it out.

Fear is just one of these aroused states of the nervous system. From a Daoist perspective, it is not a great place to spend your time. In Traditional Chinese Medicine, persistent or excessive fear has a detrimental effect on your kidneys.

All the organs of your body are related to each other energetically and their functions either support or control another organs function. Without getting into the details of the five elements and the cycles of the organs, it is worth noting that imbalances in the kidneys will have knock on effects that will further affect the emotions and nervous system.

It's worth being aware that if something goes up, it has to come down. If the nervous system is in a state of arousal, the body will put a brake on that at some point and in the return to a balanced state there may be a few swings of the emotional pendulum before coming to rest.

You do not want life to be a rollercoaster of emotions full of exciting highs and tearful lows. If your experience of life is like that, when you get off and plant your feet on the ground and attempt to ground yourself, your legs will be wobbling, knees will be knocking and your nervous system will be frazzled.

The Ideal Emotion
The ideal emotion from a Daoist perspective is contentment. This is a balanced place of serenity where your body is relaxed and your mind and emotions are calm. There is minimal stimulation of the nervous system one way or the other and a feeling of deep peace.

When your nervous system is no longer screaming at your brain and body alerting them to the wild swings of mental activity, of pleasure and displeasure, the mind opens to be able to perceive reality in a completely new way.

Daoists use physical exercises, practical philosophy and Changming to bring them to this place of serene contentment to ready themselves for the higher practises. That's right. Everything we've covered in the book so far is merely the foundation for a deeper practise that is hidden and unobtainable by those who do not work on themselves to calm and then strengthen the mind, body and spirit.

One of the first steps on this path is to eliminate fear and live fearlessly.

Once a man has vanquished fear, he is free from it for the rest of his life because, instead of fear, he has acquired clarity--a clarity of mind which erases fear.

Carlos Casteneda

The Stonecutter

There was once, a stonecutter who was dissatisfied with himself and with his position in life.

One day he passed a wealthy merchant's house. Through the open gateway, he saw many fine possessions and important visitors. "How powerful that merchant must be!" thought the stonecutter. He became very envious and wished that he could be like the merchant.

To his great surprise, he suddenly became the merchant, enjoying more luxuries and power than he had ever imagined, but envied and detested by those less wealthy than himself. Soon a high official passed by, carried in a sedan chair, accompanied by attendants and escorted by soldiers beating gongs. Everyone, no matter how wealthy, had to bow low before the procession. "How powerful that official is!" he thought. "I wish that I could be a high official!"

Then he became the high official, carried everywhere in his embroidered sedan chair, feared and hated by the people all around. It was a hot summer day, so the official felt very uncomfortable in the sticky sedan chair. He looked up at the sun. It shone proudly in the sky, unaffected by his presence. "How powerful the sun is!" he thought. "I wish that I could be the sun!"

Then he became the sun, shining fiercely down on everyone, scorching the fields, cursed by the farmers and labourers. However, a huge black cloud moved between him and the earth, so that his light could no longer shine on everything below. "How powerful that storm cloud is!" he thought. "I wish that I could be a cloud!"

Then he became the wind, blowing tiles off the roofs of houses, uprooting trees, feared and hated by all below him. Nevertheless, after a while, he ran up against something that would not move, no matter how forcefully he blew against it – a huge, towering rock. "How powerful that rock is!" he thought. "I wish that I could be a rock!"

Then he became the rock, more powerful than anything else on Earth. However, as he stood there, he heard the sound of a hammer pounding a chisel into the hard surface, and felt himself being changed. "What could be more powerful than I, the rock?" he thought.

He looked down and saw far below him the figure of a stonecutter."

The Bells

Cultivating a fearless approach to life is not easy in today's hectic world. However, we must accept the world the way it is. It is no good if you can only achieve contentment and happiness when you remove yourself from the world, submerged in a scented candle-lit bath. Our contentment has to be so strongly embodied in us that the crazy modern life simply cannot affect us.

Our teacher uses the example of standing beside a huge cast iron bell. When you begin your training, things will happen in life that might upset you. A bill you can't pay comes through the door, you lose something important to you, your girlfriend or boyfriend leaves you. Each of these is like the bell tolling loudly and the deafening vibrations shaking you into a place of fear and worry.

As you begin to train and strengthen yourself, it is as if a layer of fabric like a towel is placed over the bell. Bills still come through the door, you lose things you need, people let you down but the noise is not so deafening and the vibrations not so jagged.

Year by year the thickness of the fabric covering gets thicker and thicker until even when "negative" events occur, the vibration is muffled and they barely register, no longer upset you and have no power to unbalance your peaceful state of being. You begin to experience what it is like to live a fearless life.

Crocs
This makes you a very powerful person in a world where most people are emotionally unhinged and flying off the handle at the merest tinkle of a doorbell.

As you are able to develop and cultivate this feeling more and more you will find yourself disengaging from the emotion of mainstream news, entertainment, office politics and gossip. If this doesn't happen naturally, you should make it a conscious decision.

The mainstream media aims to shock and stimulate your nervous system at every turn. Keeping you addicted to this emotional puppet dance is in their interest but not in yours. They play on the fears and insecurities of the most primitive part of your brain, the amygdala, sometimes referred to as the reptile brain.

Wray Herbert in his article 'Fleeing the Brain's Fear Center'[20] says that according to a thorough review of the vast literature on amygdala function, the amygdala appears initially to evaluate the relevance of stimuli, and then to tune the individual's overall cognitive and emotional response.

Essentially, it checks what is happening around us and then decides whether to fight, flee or linger.

---

[20]www.psychologicalscience.org/news/full-frontal-psychology/fleeing-the-brains-fear-center.html#.WTPI_mjys1J

Mainstream news shows us the worst, scariest, most threatening events going on in the world and is like a constant needle pricking our reptile brain to respond with a squirt of adrenaline to the system.

So incredibly seldom are the events a genuine threat to your wellbeing or safety, but the perceived threat is enough to trigger this physical response.

Cut this out. It's doing you no good at all.

Heavenly Gates

As you start to cultivate the feeling of fearlessness and spend more time in a serene state, you will start to regard this as precious. You will want to protect yourself from the disturbing vibrations of the media or others who are addicted to the emotional rollercoaster.

Instead you will seek solitude or surround yourself with others who embody the feeling too. Together with others, you can magnify this energy so that it exists not just in you but in the energy, you and others emit. Together you will be able to create an environment that differs from everyday experience. Others on the path who are seeking refuge from the craziness of life will sense this and be drawn towards you.

Through your example, you will be able to teach them and affirm that there is another way. We can live in this crazy world and find harmony within it.

As you become stronger still, you will be able to transmit this feeling to anyone who you meet. Even the most aggressive, unhappy, hostile person will soften and relax in your presence. Negative emotions and interpersonal conflict disappear.

In Daoism, this is called 'Creating Heaven on Earth'. Through their practises, Daoists cultivate this feeling as very real. They don't need or want to shout about it or convince others. They live in heaven whilst still here on earth. Those who want to and those who are meant to will find a way to join them. Those who aren't, won't.

CHAPTER 14
Three Lishi Exercises

EXERCISE 1
Vertical Planking

The alignment of the spine is crucial to the development of the Daoist body in Lishi. To strengthen the muscles that support the spine and to develop an awareness of correct posture we use a lengthening process that helps open the energy gates of the body and promote the flow of qi. In China, they call it "Stand like a Pole" (Like a Maypole, not like a person from Poland).

This exercise is better done with the assistance of a partner as shown in the video at www.lishi.org/wayout but you can also practise on your own to start with.

STAGE ONE
Stand in bear stance with your bum stuck out so that there is a hollow in your lower back (lumbar). Use your abdominal muscles to roll your pelvis forwards and tuck your sacral curve and bum under whilst pushing the lower back (lumbar) so that the hollow becomes flat.

Relax and let your bum stick out again and repeat the movement.

Repeat ten times. If you have a partner who can help with this ask them to place the flat of their fist in the hollow of your lower back and provide you with a gentle pressure to push against as you roll the pelvis under and straighten the lower back.

STAGE TWO

Keeping the lower back flat, we now move our attention up the spine to a point opposite your sternum and in-between your shoulder blades (thoracic curve).

Start by sticking the chest out and rolling the shoulders back a bit like an army sergeant. This should create a bit of a hollow in the upper back.

Keeping the lower back flat, roll the shoulders forwards slightly and energise the point between the shoulder blades so that the hollow disappears and the thoracic curve becomes straight.

Repeat ten times.

If you have a partner whom can help with this ask them to place the flat of their fist in the hollow between your shoulder blades and provide you with a gentle pressure to push against as you roll the pelvis under and straighten the lower back.

STAGE THREE

Keeping both the lower and upper back flat and aligned, we move now to a point at the base of the neck (C7 of the cervical curve).

Start by extending your chin forwards so you look a little like a chicken.

Making a circular movement, drop the chin down and then pull it inwards as you lengthen the spine and neck energising the point where your spine becomes your neck.

Repeat ten times.

If you have a partner who can help with this ask them to place the heel of their hand at the point where your spine becomes your neck and provide you with a gentle pressure to push against as you circle the chin in and lengthen the spine.

Developing a strong backbone ensures that the openness of your heart, your relaxed countenance and playful attitude to life are supported by a firm foundation of power. The alignment of the spine in this way promotes strong energy flow, resilience and a confidence in who you are and how you choose to live your life.

When you know that you have strength behind you, it is easier to live a fearless life.

EXERCISE 2
Happy Days

This Dao Yin respiration therapy exercise combines the S-Breathe with an expansive full body stretch. It revitalises the whole body and is great for your circulation. It is called Happy Days and if you make it a regular practise, that is exactly what you will experience.

By expanding your body to its maximum height and width whilst using your breath to extend your energy all around you, you create an unseen buffer that protects you and supports you to move through life in a fearless manner.

Stand in eagle stance with your heels touching and your feet forming a 90° angle to each other so that one foot points to 2 o'clock and the other to 10 o'clock (Northeast and North-West if that makes more sense). We have recorded a video, which is available at www.lishi.org/wayout

BREATHE IN
Cross your left arm over your right as you bring both arms across your torso, lifting up to your chest and uncrossing as you reach up above your head. At the same time as your arms lift up, raise up on to your tiptoes keeping the heels touching in the air.

BREATHE OUT MAKING THE S-SOUND
Keep the arms straight as you lower them both to the sides of the body gradually lowering the heels back to the floor so that the little finger edge of your hands touches the outside of your thighs at the same time as your heels touch the floor.

Repeat but this time crossing the right arm on top of the left.

You can repeat these two breathes three times, five times or ten times.

Feel your lungs and body feeling with strength and power as you breathe in.

Visualise a large ball of energy surrounding you and extending in all directions as you breathe out.

Enjoy the buzz.

By doing this exercise you strengthen your lungs which initiates a constructive cycle that in-turn supports your kidneys. Fear as an emotion weakens the kidneys. Supporting them in this way helps in the quest to live a fearless life.

EXERCISE 3
Dancing

Emotion and motion are connected. Movement is a powerful tool for shifting us out of negative emotions, and into states of pleasure and enjoyment of life. Dancing is a wonderful way to connect with your body; simply enjoy owning and moving it, however you like.

The free expression of your energy through physical movement is a source of fear for many people. They feel embarrassed or say they are "not a good dancer". Their fears of being judged or their act of judging themselves harshly triggers emotions and tightens their bodies.

It's time to release them and take a tangible step towards a fearless life.

If you haven't danced for a while then put on some of your favourite music and have a little boogie now. It doesn't have to be for long. A few minutes should do it, you'll be feeling fine, and dandy lickety split.

The Daoists recognise the effect that movement has on our overall health and wellbeing and developed hundreds of different forms, sets and dances to harness these benefits. Within Lishi, we have a particular dance that is called Flying Hands. It is a sequence of nearly two-hundred moves linked together in a wonderfully expansive, circular whirlwind of expression. It takes years to learn but feels fantastic to do.

It is far too complicated a task to try to teach you the Flying Hands of Lishi in this book so we urge you to find a qualified Lishi teacher. www.lishi.org/classes will tell you where your nearest one is.

Whether it's the Flying Hands dance or jumping around to your favourite tunes, make dance a regular part of your life and allow the movement to rid you of stale or stuck emotions and lift your spirits to a higher vibration.

CHAPTER 15
Three Changming Lifestyle Recommendations

CHANGMING 1
We Are Social Creatures
So Get To a Class

Daoism is not a head game. It is not about reading flowery texts and fantasising that you are an immortal. It is not about hiding from or running away from the real world it is about becoming strong and being able to enjoy navigating through it as you lift yourself to a higher quality of experience.

There is even a branch of Daoism called Quanzhen, which is the 'Complete Reality' school.

Other people are a part of reality. The energy of civilisation is the combined interaction of the billions of people on this planet. Learning to be comfortable, enjoy and be skilful with the energy of our fellow human beings is a key stage in our path of development.

For many people, social situations are a source of great anxiety and fear. Make sure that you venture out from your cave from time to time and mix with other like-minded folk. Find a Lishi class near you and meet others walking a similar path. Learn from them and enjoy their company and comradery.

If there isn't a Lishi class near you find another activity to ensure that there is a social element to your training and your life.

Switch off your TV, pack up your games console, unplug from the virtual world from time to time and enter the real world for a fully connected energy adventure. Embrace the fear. Eat the fear. Release the fear.

The ancient Daoists didn't have TV and films to distract themselves from their practise. There wasn't a lot to do and so their focus on their training was all-encompassing. Don't get the wrong idea though. We're not saying that it's never OK to enjoy a bit of digital fantasy. We love sitting down for a couple or three episodes of our favourite series as much as the next person does.

It's important to realise that too much entertainment is a distraction. We have to maintain our practise in the real world if we are going to do as the old Daoists have done for millennia and ensure that Daoism is real and not just something that people read about in books.

Meet people and connect with them energetically. It is hugely nourishing to be with and enjoy the company of others. Socialising and having fun is part of the richness of life but as mentioned earlier seek out and surround yourself with like-minded people who are going to nourish you and support you on your journey.

Share your experience of life with others. Maybe you are in a relationship, maybe you are not. Don't worry about that. As you work on yourself and become a stronger, softer, more loving and content person you will become more attractive and will get to enjoy physical, mental, even spiritual connections with others.

Do things that stimulate and nourish you physically, emotionally and mentally and include others in those experiences. Develop deep and rich friendships with people.

Be willing to be vulnerable. That is where you will learn that there is nothing to fear and how you will inspire others to do the same.

CHANGMING 2
Simplify Your Life

We've all heard the phrase that "Less is more" but do we really believe it? To start to really appreciate the truth of this statement begin eliminating elements in your life that are unessential. Spend more time doing what is important to you and less time doing things that are a bit, well meh!

You don't owe anything to anyone really other than yourself and being true to your path. That doesn't mean it's OK to shaft people over but it does mean that it's OK to take a time out, focus on what makes you happy and disconnect from people or activities that no longer nourish you.

Learn to slow down in everything that you do. Instead of wolfing your food down, chew it slowly and really appreciate every mouthful. When you drive, be more present and considerate and in less of a hurry. When you talk to your kids, your partner, or your friends, put away your phone, slow down and listen. Really connect with them and be with them. Enjoy the moments of life instead of distracting yourself or rushing to the next one.

Declutter. Own less. It always feels good mentally to get rid of junk and things that lay dormant and stagnant in your living space. If you haven't used something or worn it in the last 12 months then it can definitely be released.

Notice if you hold any fear around letting things go. Instead, learn to trust that everything you need will come to you as and when you need it.

Eat well. Enjoy healthy meals. Often this just involves simplifying what you buy and eat. Buy the raw ingredients and learn to cook healthy wholesome food.

It's simple to do and enjoyable to learn and makes you a much better catch in the eyes of a potential partner, boy or girl.

To attain knowledge, add things every day. To attain wisdom, remove things every day.

Laozi

Rather than buying sugary, salt laden, de-natured foods that upset the balance of the kidneys, go for the vibrant, vital, fresh, organic fruit and veg. The more vital the food you eat, the more energy you will have to achieve what you want in life.

Foods that are particularly nourishing to the kidneys and therefore helpful at reducing fear include grapes, plums, boysenberries, celery, turnips, watercress, asparagus, millet, endive, cabbage, black beans, amaranth, rye, barley, quinoa, oats, kelp, nori, chlorella, miso, cinnamon, dill seed, and chives.

Live debt free. It is too easy in the modern world to become lured into a black hole of debt. Money is just another form of energy and learning how to work with it and make it work for you is another form of qigong.

Companies and banks will offer you overdrafts and credit and make it seem easy to get what you want. They are masters in the art of enslaving you.

They have been doing it for centuries are immensely sophisticated and hugely powerful institutions. As a result, debt and money issues are a huge source of fear for many people.

Don't be a sucker. Live within your means and build your reserves. Learn how money works and get it to work for you instead of being trapped into working for it. Consumer debt adds stress to your life, erodes our power and steals our freedom. Stay free and master money.

Prioritise your time over money. We all need money to live and exist in the modern world but don't make money your only goal in life.

A man is successful if he gets up in the morning and gets to bed at night and in between does whatever he wants to do

Bob Dylan

Be like Bob.

CHANGMING 3
Kidney Beans

Your Kidneys are two bean-shaped organs, each one roughly the size of your fist. In Traditional Chinese Medicine, in addition to the function they form of filtering the blood and removing excess fluid and other waste, they are also linked to the sexual energies and the emotions of fear and will-power.

Deficient Kidney Qi, or energy, can cause feelings of extreme or persistent anxiety or even panic attacks. These conditions could also be a sign that your Kidney and Heart are not functioning in harmony.

When the heart is balanced, you feel at peace. We want the heart to be balanced and we aim to be in a state of peace. When the heart is out of balance, people feel restless, confused, fidgety and unable to sleep.

Because TCM views Kidney Qi as the energy foundation for the entire body, the best way to address emotional issues like this is to treat their root cause by strengthening Kidney Qi.

The Changming principle that is key to supporting this on a daily basis is to 'Eat like a King in the morning, a Prince at Lunch and a Pauper at dinner'. What this means is that breakfast should be your biggest meal, lunch should be less hearty but still provide fuel and then your evening meal should be light.

When your body is well fed, it will support you to execute on the activities of the day. If you just start the day with a Pop Tart and a coffee, your body will quite rightly be nervous about whether it is going to get the nutrition it needs.

Having a hearty breakfast, grounds and centres your energy, and provides a firm base for a fearless day.

Working with the 24-hour body clock outlined in Chapter Six this ensures that you take advantage of when the digestive system has most energy and that you don't overload the digestive system and liver late at night.

To support the digestive system and by extension the heart it is recommended to eat mainly cooked foods. Cooking foods makes it easier to digest and extract the energy whereas cold, raw foods are considered too yin to be consumed regularly. They are too cooling for the stomach and leach energy that could be used in better ways.

Finally, aim to chew your foods as much as you can. Ideally chew until each mouthful is liquid. Your teeth have then done most of the heavy lifting and your stomach can have an easier time of it. If you don't have the patience to chew to liquid, pick a number between 30 and 50 chews and make sure you chew that many times before swallowing.

In taking care of your digestive system in this way it will better support your kidneys, strengthen your will power and help you be in the state of fearlessness we have been talking about in this chapter.

SUMMARY

So there you have it. The Daoist path to a fearless life by following the principles of the Lishi lifestyle. These involve guarding the three treasures of compassion, humility and frugality and aligning your own values with these time-tested shortcuts to happiness.

Fearlessness is achieved by encouraging your inner child to come out and play so you maintain a childlike energy and express your inner nature without fear or judgement.

We shared some exercises that strengthen your ability to have happy days, powerfully back up your childlike and loving approach to life as well as dance yourself free of your fears.

Finally, the healthy living guidelines of Changming encourage us to get social and connect with others, simplify our lives and make simple changes that strengthen the physical organ of our kidneys.

Adopting these practices will transform your experience so that your familiarity and understanding of what fearlessness is will deepen and deepen.

In the next and final chapter, we will offer suggestions for how you can take everything that you have learned so far and integrate it into your personal Lishi lifestyle.

Walking the Path

Most Daoist texts written by academics in the West give readers intellectual theories of Daoist practice, which are wonderful in conveying the ideas and concepts within Daoism. That is where it ends; there is no practical methodology of achieving what you are reading about.

However, Daoism is not an intellectual exercise. It's not something that you read about in a book as an abstract idea or philosophy that makes you feel good. It is a very much a daily practise. The Daoist Arts that we practise and that we have outlined in this book, when lived on a daily basis, we call the Lishi Lifestyle.

If the Lishi lifestyle appeals to you then there are a number of things that you can do to make it part of how you live. The most important thing to do is to find a teacher. Depending on where you are in the world, this will be either easy or difficult.

We have a number of very good teachers (who have trained for at least 10 years) at locations in the UK, France, Germany, Holland, Tenerife, Mexico, USA and China. We also have a number of teachers who travel and offer workshops at locations where we don't have regular classes.

Unfortunately, there are a great many locations where we don't have regular classes and so we have developed resources to help people get started on this journey.

In this final section, we outline a training plan for people who aren't lucky enough to have a Lishi class on their doorstep. You can find out where your nearest class is by visiting www.lishi.org/classes

CHAPTER 16
The Way Out Training Plan

We have covered a lot in this book and you might be keen to start a training ritual for yourself but aren't sure where to start. To help, we've outlined two possible plans depending on whether you want to take a relaxed approach or a more intense approach to getting started. Both plans refer to the exercises we have covered throughout this book.

	RELAXED
Day 1	Gentle Warm up 1 Direction Breathing x 4 Standing Qigong for 1 minute Square Yard Taiji
Day 2	Gentle Warm up 1 Direction Breathing x 4 Standing Qigong for 1 minute Square Yard Taiji
Day 3	Gentle Warm up 1 Direction Breathing x 4 Happy Days Dao Yin x 3 Vertical Planking Standing Qigong for 90 seconds Square Yard Taiji

Day 4	Gentle Warm up 1 Direction Breathing x 4 Vertical Planking Happy Days Dao Yin x 5 Standing Qigong for 90 seconds Square Yard Taiji
Day 5	Gentle Warm up 1 Direction Breathing x 4 Vertical Planking Happy Days Dao Yin x 5 Standing Qigong for 90 seconds Square Yard Taiji
Day 6	Gentle Warm up 1 Direction Breathing x 4 Vertical Planking Happy Days Dao Yin x 5 Standing Qigong for 2 minutes Square Yard Taiji
Day 7	Relax, chill with friends and read some Daoist Texts. Do the Inner Smile Exercise.

	INTENSIVE
Day 1	Gentle Warm up 1 Direction Breathing x 4 Vertical Planking Happy Days Dao Yin x 3 Standing Qigong for 2 minutes Square Yard Taiji
Day 2	Gentle Warm up 1 Direction Breathing x 4 Vertical Planking Happy Days Dao Yin x 3 Standing Qigong for 2 minutes Square Yard Taiji
Day 3	Gentle Warm up 1 Direction Breathing x 4 Vertical Planking Happy Days Dao Yin x 5 Standing Qigong for 2 ½ minutes Square Yard Taiji

Day 4	Gentle Warm up
	1 Direction Breathing x 4
	Vertical Planking
	Happy Days Dao Yin x 5
	Standing Qigong for 2 ½ minutes
	Square Yard Taiji
Day 5	Gentle Warm up
	1 Direction Breathing x 4
	Vertical Planking
	Happy Days Dao Yin x 7
	Standing Qigong for 2 ½ minutes
	Square Yard Taiji
Day 6	Gentle Warm up
	1 Direction Breathing x 4
	Vertical Planking
	Happy Days Dao Yin x 7
	Standing Qigong for 3 minutes
	Square Yard Taiji
Day 7	Relax, chill with friends and read some Daoist Texts. Do the Inner Smile Exercise.

Online Video Course for Beginners

The best way to get started if you don't have a teacher near you is to sign up for our online video course for beginners. You will find this at: www.lishi.org/highenergytaichi

In this course, Wai-Yii will lead you through some of the foundations of Lishi. She will cover the warm-up, the different stances we use, how to breathe, some Dao Yin respiration therapy exercises, some Dao Yoga and the first sequences of the Taiji form and Flying Hands dance.

You can repeat the course on a weekly basis until you have learned the moves and can practise them yourself without following the videos. In time, we will develop additional courses that will allow you to deepen your practise and extend your knowledge of Lishi.

The Basic Changming Cookbook

As you have learned in this book, a healthy diet is a key part of Daoist practise. We have compiled a simple recipe book that introduces you to some of the basics of sourcing, preparing and cooking the Changming way.

There are close to 60 recipes covering Soups, Mains and Desserts and it is available on kindle by searching for "The Basic Changming Cookbook" on your local amazon website[21]. We also plan to run some Changming Cookery Courses too so get in touch if that sounds like something you'd like to learn.

Since learning to cook and eat the Changming way is such an important and enjoyable part of the Lishi lifestyle, it is worth making a start with this alongside your physical practise.

---

[21] You will find English and German versions.

Remember, Changming is an art too. It is not a fad and will take you time to fully appreciate and integrate into your life.

Please don't be too strict or rigid but instead enjoy the process of learning about the effect of foods on your body and energies.

As you begin to make the connection between your health and emotions and the foods you consume you will gain an awareness and a power that few people fully appreciate. Rather than wolfing down fast food whilst on the go or devouring glutinously rich fattening foods, you will start to appreciate the simple flavours and turn meals into mindful exercise that further centres and grounds you. You will become stronger, calmer and more content.

Connect With Other Lishi Practitioners
We have a number of ways that you can connect with other Lishi practitioners across the globe via social media. It is a vibrant community and teachers and students alike share tips and news about what they are up to or opportunities to train or learn more about Lishi.

We are most active on Facebook and Instagram.

You can find us at:
Our Facebook Page: facebook.com/lishileedstaichi
Our Facebook Group: Facebook.com/lishileedsdaoisttaichi
Instagram.com/lishiarts
Twitter.com/lishiarts

You can connect with Lishi International and the International Daoist Society at:
Facebook.com/Lishi.org and
Facebook.com/like.lishi

If you search social media for Lishi, you will find a number of other teachers in locations around the world who regularly post interesting things related to the Lishi lifestyle.

We also blog regularly and you can read our blog at lishi.org/blog/waiyii/

The Lishi International blog can be found at lishi.org/blog

Create a Portal near You
In Leeds, we have weekly classes that are portals to a high-energy lifestyle. They are places that people can come on a weekly basis or more often to be a part of the Lishi Community. Attending regularly lifts your energy and teaches you how to access and maintain a high-energy experience of life.

If you are keen to experience this near you then I am sure there is a way. If you start to practise Lishi using the above resources and can generate interest amongst your community, then get in touch.

If you have people interested and can organise a venue where we could run a weekend course, then contact us and we'll do our best to come and visit.

In the near future, we hope to be able to invite you into our classes in Leeds via live video streaming.

Become a Member
The governing body for the arts of Lishi is The International Daoist Society. It is a UK charity with members around the world. If you would like to support the work that we do and contribute to the development and sharing of Lishi and the Daoist Arts then we encourage you to become a member.

You can join online at www.lishi.org/membership

Membership gives you a number of benefits and opens up additional opportunities to dive deeper into the practise of Daoism including the opportunity to train at courses run by our teacher, the Grand Master of the system.

Daoist Centre

We are good friends with the White Cloud Temple in Beijing and they have asked us to establish a Daoist Centre in the UK. It is likely to be in London initially with smaller branches opening elsewhere in time.

It will be a space for anyone with an interest in the Daoist Arts to come and learn, practise and be part of the Daoist community. We will host Daoist experts from all over the world who will share their knowledge at special events and retreats.

The first step is to find a space within an existing venue in London. In time, we will look for our own dedicated premises. If you can help us at all then please do get in touch.

You can follow the journey at facebook.com/seacloudtemple and lishi.org/temple

Join us on a Winter Retreat in Tenerife

During the cold winter months we head off somewhere hot and sunny to work on our tans and train in the heat. If you'd like to join us and meet like-minded people learning Lishi (Taiji, Detox Breathing, Dao Yoga, Meditation, Life Coaching and Changming Cookery), register your interest at:
www.lishi.org/events and we will send you all the details of the next retreat we will be running.

Personal Lishi Lifestyle Coaching

You are unique and so is your ideal lifestyle. Lishi Lifestyle Coaching is a comprehensive one-to-one coaching programme that will allow you to create your ideal path through life using the Daoist principles of Lishi. The programme will take you step-by-step from where you are now to the life you want to lead.

A fusion of ancient Daoist principles, cutting-edge coaching technologies and a structured method for identifying and walking your path guarantees that you will move closer to living your ideal lifestyle on a physical, mental, emotional and spiritual level.

This is a higher ticket item and not for everybody. Places are strictly limited and you will need to complete an application form and attend a telephone interview for one of the few slots we open each year.

If you sense that this might be for you then get in touch and we can start the application process to find out if this will be a good fit.

SUMMARY

In this chapter, we outlined ways that you can continue your journey into Lishi. We recognise that it is not an easy path if you are not located close to one of our trained teachers so we have developed a number of resources to support you.

We offer you two syllabi for your training based on the exercises covered in this book. If you start to use these as a structure for your training, you will quickly feel the benefits. You will also become eager to learn more and to deepen your practise.

Please practise safely, stay grounded and try not to rush. Keep working on the basics and your body and your energies will reveal important lessons to you. In time, you will want and need additional guidance. The resources we have offered in this chapter will be a start and perhaps the Dao will bring you to Leeds or to another location where we have classes and your training can progress to a new level.

We have covered a tremendous amount in these pages and your head is probably spinning. You may have many questions and feel a need to re-visit some sections of the book. We hope you feel able to dip back in to the book whenever you need an answer.

Wherever you are on your journey, the principles, exercises and practises are enormously beneficial if you can apply them and embody them in your life.

We offer them as a road map to guide you or a menu from which you can choose. Depending on what you are working on, you have in your hands a resource that will help you to be natural, cope with stress, find your flow, get what you want and live a fearless life.

We trust that you have found value in these pages and we hope that you will take what you have learned and apply it in your life.

Use the wisdom of Way Out and turn it into a daily practise for your life. If you are diligent and sincere and adhere to the principles outlined then you will not only live harmoniously in these crazy times but you will also thrive and ultimately experience life, as it should be, as heaven on earth.

We wish you well on your journey and should the Dao ordain that our paths cross, we look forward to hearing how you found your Way Out and how it has changed your life for the better.

Be well.

Love Wai-Yii and Ben

ACKNOWLEDGEMENTS

We have had the help of many people in creating this book.

Our many students, who have asked us questions, shared with us what they have gained from practising Lishi and repeatedly requested us to write a book. Thank you for inspiring us to put pen to paper in the first place.

Thank you to Samantha Toolsie from Toolsie Photography for a fun few hours taking headshots for the back page and our website.

Thanks to the talented designer, Helen Wilson, for her patience and skill at transforming our ideas into a beautiful cover.

A big, big thank you to our teacher, Laoba for sharing wisdom that has changed our lives. This book would not exist without the years of transmission of the principles and practices as well as the living exemplar you are of the Lishi Daoist system.

pg 25 - resource website

CPSIA information can be obtained
at www.ICGtesting.com
Printed in the USA
FSHW011950010421
80089FS